PRINCIPLES OF
VIOLIN
PLAYING & TEACHING

Ivan Galamian

PRINCIPLES OF
VIOLIN
PLAYING & TEACHING

third edition

Ivan Galamian

with a postscript by
Elizabeth A. H. Green
Professor Emeritus (Music)
The University of Michigan

SHAR PRODUCTS COMPANY
P.O. Box 1411 Ann Arbor, Michigan 48106

Galamian, Ivan.
  Principles of Violin Playing & Teaching.

ISBN 0-9621416-4-X
LCCN 99-62988

Printed in Ann Arbor, Michigan (USA)
10 9

ISBN   0-9621416-4-X

Prentice-Hall International (UK) Limited, *London*
Prentice-Hall of Australia Pty. Limited, *Sydney*
Prentice-Hall Canada Inc., *Toronto*
Prentice-Hall Hispanoamiericana, S. A., *Mexico*
Prentice-Hall of India Private Limited, *New Delhi*
Prentice-Hall of Japan, Inc., *Tokyo*
Simon & Schuster Asia Pte. Ltd., *Singapore*
Editora Prentice-Hall do Brasil, Ltda., *Rio de Janeiro*

I have lived in the era of the world's great pedagogues. No man has contributed so much to the art of violin playing in the last fifty years as has Ivan Galamian. He was a wonderful human being, devoted to his students and friends, and, to those who knew him intimately, he represented the ideal in Music and in Life.

JOSEF GINGOLD

Nothing could give me greater pleasure than to write a few words about my teacher, Ivan Galamian. He was a virtuoso teacher whose system of teaching the violin was both ingenious and logical. He applied that system to all of his students, and it worked, no matter how much or how little talent the student had—a true sign of a great pedagogue.

This book, *Principles of Violin Playing and Teaching*, gives us a wonderful insight into Mr. Galamian's very special method of teaching the violin and I am sure that it will be of great benefit to the readers. I am delighted that this book is being reissued, not only for the benefit of countless violin students, but also because it is a fitting tribute to Mr. Galamian's lifelong work.

ITZHAK PERLMAN

TABLE OF CONTENTS

CONCERNING
THE SECOND EDITION

Two things should be said about the second edition. First, the original writing, as given in the first edition, is preserved *in toto*. Second, the new material has been added in three chapters at the end. It is cross-referenced throughout and presents "the other side of the coin"—*how* Mr. Galamian revolutionized our thinking, our practicing, and our total performance during that magic hour each week in the studio.

The summer school at Meadowmount (near Elizabethtown, New York) was equipped with fully edited master copies of all works studied. Mr. Galamian would suggest that we edit our own copies therefrom so that lesson time would not be wasted. Only minor adaptations to the individual student needed to be added in the studio lessons. The material in Part III of the Postscript, the "Glossary of Applied Variations," is taken from personal copies of the edited Meadowmount books. Unless otherwise stated, quotation marks refer to Mr. Galamian's words.

Sincere appreciation is extended to the following colleagues, whose assistance and dedication to the memory of our admired and respected teacher accounts for the accuracy and completeness of the added chapters:

Professor David Cerone, who has taken over Mr. Galamian's duties on the faculty at Curtis Institute and continues the Galamian tradition at Meadowmount; Michael Avsharian, Jr., private teacher, associated with Mr. Galamian for some twenty years and a member of the Meadowmount faculty from 1960-

66; Sally Thomas and Margaret Pardee-Butterly, long-time faculty colleagues of Mr. Galamian, both at Meadowmount and at Juilliard; and finally, Charles Avsharian, Adjunct Professor of Violin at The University of Michigan, to whom we owe the series of video tapes showing Mr. Galamian's studio teaching during the summers of 1979 and 1980.

This new edition goes to press with the blessing of Mrs. Ivan Galamian (Judith Johnson Galamian) whose business efficiency over the years freed her husband to dedicate his life to his students.

Ann Arbor   *Elizabeth A. H. Green*

PREFACE
TO THE FIRST EDITION

There are many systems of violin playing, some good, some fair, some bad. The system that I have tried to present in the following pages is the one that I believe to be the most practical, but I do not contend that it is the only right or only possible one.

Putting a system into a book, even writing a book like this, is a problematical undertaking because no printed work can ever replace the live teacher-student relationship. The very best that a teacher can give to a student is the individualized, unique approach, which is too personal a thing to be put down on paper anyway.

The actual writing of this book has taken many years. It was begun at the gentle urging of several of my students whose faith in the project has kept it alive. The first seven years were given over to the collecting of data from lessons in the studio and to the making of the first complete draft of the work. The copy for this first draft was prepared by Miss Elizabeth Green of the University of Michigan faculty. During the next two years the book underwent several changes in format and one complete revision. In the tenth year Miss Green resumed work on the project in order to complete the final manuscript which, in time, became the book you now hold in your hands. I should like to express my appreciation for her long interest in this project.

Nobody can study, nobody can teach from a book alone. What a book can do is to help. It can do so by mapping out the general principles as such, and by trying to clarify many of the problems involved. Whether the efforts expended herein have been successful, only the conscientious reader will be able to judge.

Before proceeding to the body of the work, I wish to thank Mr. Gustave Rosseels for reading the final manuscript and also to acknowledge the valuable assistance rendered by Dr. Frederick Neumann of the University of Richmond faculty.

New York   *Ivan Galamian*

Introduction

DEFICIENCIES OF SOME
PRESENT-DAY SYSTEMS

Many things are being taught by the various present-day methods that I would not care to endorse. For the moment, I shall limit myself to the singling out of three major items. I do so because they are common to almost every system of violin playing and also because they concern the very foundation of all violin teaching.

The first of these is the contemporary insistence upon compliance with rigid rules for everyone and everything that has to do with violin playing. The making of rigid rules is a dangerous procedure, since rules as such should be made for the good of the students rather than using the students to glorify the rules.

In violin playing, as in any other art, that which can be formulated is not a set of unyielding rules but rather a group of general principles that are broad enough to cover all cases, yet flexible enough to be applied to any particular case. The teacher must realize that every student is an individual with his own personality, his own characteristic physical and mental make-up, his own approach to the instrument and to music. Once the teacher recognizes this, he must treat the student accordingly. Naturalness should be his first guiding principle. "Right" is only what is natural for the particular student, for only what is natural is comfortable and efficient. The efforts of the teacher, therefore, must be devoted to making every student as comfortable as possible with the instrument. In this connection it is distressing to think of the many unnatural theories of technique which have come and gone—and of the new ones which still keep on coming—that have forced students into a constant struggle against Nature herself and consequently against a natural approach to the instrument. Such a battle has never yet been won by anybody.

The obsession for rigid rules with their resultant disregard for the principle of naturalness gives us our first concern.

The second, which is closely related to the first, is the failure to realize that however important the individual elements in violin technique are, more important still is the understanding of their *interdependence* in a mutual, organic relationship. If, to give an example, the bow is held after one fashion, then the functioning of the fingers, hand, wrist, and arm will fall into a certain organic pattern. If the bow-grip is changed, one must permit all other parts of the hand and arm to find their corresponding organic adjustment and their new natural balance, one with the other. The teacher should be prepared to deal with such differences in action pattern from one individual to another by making compromises to fit the particular student. Such adjustments are a personal thing. They cannot be formulated into rigid rules for all players.

Thirdly, I would like to point to the one-sided overemphasis on the purely physical and mechanical aspects of violin technique, the ignoring of the fact that what is paramount in importance is not the physical movements as such but the *mental control over them*. The key to facility and accuracy and, ultimately, to complete mastery of violin technique is to be found in the *relationship of mind to muscles*, that is, in the ability to make the sequence of mental command and physical response as quick and as precise as possible. Therein resides the fundamental principle of violin technique that is being overlooked and neglected by far too many players and teachers.

Chapter One
TECHNIQUE AND INTERPRETATION

Tone, pitch, and rhythm are the basic elements of all music. It is only logical, then, that the technique of the violin be firmly founded on these three elements in terms of beauty of tone, accuracy of intonation, and precise control of rhythm. Technique has to combine with interpretation for successful performance, and the favorable issue of the performance depends upon the following factors:

1. The Physical Factor: consisting of (a) the anatomical make-up of the individual, in particular the shape of his fingers, hands, and arms, plus the flexibility of his muscular apparatus; (b) the physiological functioning with regard to the playing movements and the muscular actions that bring them about;

2. The Mental Factor: the ability of the mind to prepare, direct, and supervise the muscular activity;

3. The Aesthetic-emotional Factor: the capacity to understand and feel the meaning of the music, plus the innate talent to project its expressive message to the listener.

ABSOLUTE AND RELATIVE VALUES

In violin playing we have to deal with two distinct categories of values. One of these can be called the absolute or unchangeable values and the other, the relative or changeable values. As the name implies, the first category is not affected by alterations of circumstances, whereas the second category may be modified or varied by the style of the period, a change of locale, or the taste of the performer.

Among the absolute values are (a) the necessity for total technical control and (b) the requisite of completely unqualified knowledge of the music to be played in all of its details, including a thorough understanding of its harmonic and formal structure. These requirements are obviously timeless. Certainly the ability to play in tune and in rhythm and to produce all of the varieties of tone colors and bowings likewise can never go out of fashion. Enlarging upon this, even though a tone color produced by a certain type of vibrato might be contrary to the taste of a particular place or time (might not be in style or in fashion), the *ability to produce it* cannot become obsolete, and, thus, it has a definite place within the inventory of the absolute values of a complete technical equipment.

Conversely, the relative values deal with the interpretive side of the performance. Interpretation, as the word itself implies, contains a strong subjective element, namely, the performer's personal conception of what the music should sound like. Since this subjective element is vitally influenced by taste, style, and fashion (which all vary from individual to individual, from place to place, and from one period to another), interpretation has to be classified as a changeable value.

The music of Bach serves as an example. If we knew (which we do not) exactly how Bach wanted his music to sound, there still would remain the question of whether it should be played precisely in the historical style of Bach's day, or whether the style should be adapted to fit modern ideas, means, and surroundings. This is a highly controversial question, and no conclusive answer is possible. For example, I might mention the discussion about the use of spiccato in Bach's works. One school of thought condemns its use, because the bowing was supposedly unknown at the time. Another school defends the use of the spiccato with the argument that if Bach had known this bowing he would certainly have approved its use. There is no way to settle this argument. Similar controversies have been raging about other aspects of Bach interpretations, such as the use of crescendos and decrescendos (which are frowned upon by purists), as well as the use of rubato, vibrato, and so on.

This example may serve to indicate the wide scope within which individual interpretations of the same piece of music can vary from one another and also why everything that has to do with interpretation belongs, of necessity, to the relative or changeable values. In the long run, every student who aspires to the level of true artistry will have to form his own opinion, make his own choice, and take his own responsibility. Therefore, the important point, fundamentally, is that the student must become fully equipped with all of the technical tools so that his musical ideas may be fully realized.

TYPES OF TECHNIQUE

Technique is the ability to direct mentally and to execute physically all of the necessary playing movements of left and right hands, arms, and fingers. A complete technique means the development of all of the elements of the violinistic skill to the highest level. In short, it is the complete mastery over all of the potentialities of the instrument. It implies the ability to do justice, with unfailing reliability and control, to each and every demand of the most refined musical imagination. It enables the player, when he has formed an ideal concept of how any work should sound, to live up to this concept in actual performance. A technique which fulfills these ultimate requirements can be called an accomplished *interpretive technique*. It is the fundamental goal for which one must strive, because it, and it alone, opens the way to the highest artistic accomplishment.

Such a complete mastery over the technical equipment is not only necessary for the soloist who wishes to achieve his own interpretation of the music, but also, in equal measure for the player who has to yield his own ideas to those of a leader (such as the conductor of the orchestra), or who must, in playing chamber music, coordinate his playing with that of the other members of the group. Without the mastery supplied by an adequate interpretive technique, a player can neither properly lead nor properly follow.

By differentiation, one can speak also of a *virtuoso technique*, which, although a technique of brilliant execution, is nevertheless not always under complete control. The fingers will often move too fast, with an effect of great speed and extraordinary facility, but without proper rhythmical discipline. Obviously, a technique of this kind, however spectacular, is not always a fully reliable tool in the service of the interpretive ideas formed by the artist.

TECHNIQUE AND CORRELATION

The foundation upon which the building of technique rests, as mentioned shortly heretofore, lies in the correct relationship of the mind to the muscles, the smooth, quick and accurate functioning of the sequence in which the mental command elicits the desired muscular response. From here on this mental-physical relationship will be referred to as *correlation.** It is the improvement of this correlation which provides the key to technical mastery and technical control and not, as apparently is commonly believed and taught, the training and building of the muscles. What counts is not the strength of the muscles, but their responsiveness to the mental directive. The better the correlation, the greater the facility, accuracy, and reliability of the technique.

The question becomes, thus, one of how to improve the correlation. The answer is that the player has to present the mind-muscle unit with problems to solve, problems that proceed from the simple to the ever more complex. The problems best suited for this purpose are those of rhythm and coordination. They will be dealt with in some detail in the chapter On Practicing. Here it is sufficient to say that such problems may take the form of (a) a variation of time values (rhythms) which are the concern of the left hand, of (b) bowing patterns for the right hand, of (c) the combination of both of the preceding as coordination problems, and finally of (d) the superimposition of accents which may further complicate the problems to be solved. Any scale or passage that the player can perform with a great many different rhythms, accentuations and bowings is one that has been completely assimilated by the mind and muscles.

INTERPRETATION

Interpretation is the final goal of all instrumental study, its only *raison d'être*. Technique is merely the means to this end, the tool to be used in the service of artistic interpretation. For successful performance, therefore, the possession of the technical tools alone is not sufficient. In addition, the player must understand the meaning of the music thoroughly, must have creative imagination and a personal emotional approach to the work if his rendition is to be lifted above the dry and the pedantic. His personality must be neither self-effacing nor aggressively obtruding.

————

* The term correlation is perhaps not ideal inasmuch as it is most often used in connection with elements that are interdependent and on a more or less equal footing, whereas here we have to do with a relationship not between equals but between a superior (the mind) and subordinates (the muscles). Aware of this weakness, I have, nevertheless, chosen the term for the sake of simplicity and convenience.

If we ask what makes a good performer, it is pertinent to think of the qualities that make a good public speaker, because they are closely related. A good speaker is one who has a good voice, good elocution and delivery, who has something important to say and says it with authority in a way that can be understood by everyone. In analogy, a good musical performer is one whose delivery combines complete technical mastery with an interpretation understandable and convincing to everyone.

There is also another analogy. A speaker will rarely move an audience if every word, every inflection, and every gesture gives the impression of careful, studied preparation. The same words would be infinitely more impressive if they seemed to come to the speaker's mind in the very moment at which they are uttered, and if the intonation of his voice, his pauses, his gestures, and all other features of his delivery seem to be genuinely and spontaneously prompted by the thoughts he expresses at the time. In other words, the less rehearsed the speech sounds, the more effective it will be.

The same holds true of the musician. The best performance always partakes of the nature of an improvisation in which the artist is moved by the music he plays, forgets about technique, and abandons himself with improvisatory freedom to the inspiration of the moment. A performance of this nature is the only one which is capable of transmitting the essence of the music to the listener with the immediacy of a true re-creation. On the other hand, the player who studies in advance how to achieve the *impression* of a certain emotion by figuring out every shake of the vibrato, by mathematically calculating every nuance, by planning according to an exact time-table every rubato so that there can be no "improvisatory nonsense"—such a player substitutes a synthetic feeling, a mechanically contrived facsimile of an emotion, for genuine inspiration. He may deceive the ear of the auditors as to the nature of this procedure but he will never deceive their emotions. The public as a whole may not have a profound reasoning power on such matters, but it has an uncanny instinct for what is genuine and what is not.

Naturally, the improvisational element must not be overdone, and a player who is not yet musically and technically matured must beware of letting his emotions run wild during a performance. Also, the improvisation has to remain within the framework of an over-all plan so that it will always do justice to the elements of style and the formal structure of the work being played. Freedom of interpretation can be soundly based only on a complete technical mastery over the means of expression.

Interpretation, in its best artistic sense, cannot be taught directly, because only a personal, creative approach is truly artistic. One that is derived, second-hand, from the teacher cannot come under the heading of genuinely creative art. It is, therefore, a great mistake for a teacher to impose his own interpretation upon all of his students. From an early age in the student's development the teacher should try to encourage a personal initiative while at the same time constantly strive to better the student's understanding and to improve his taste and sense of style. *The teacher must always bear in mind that the highest goal should be for him to make the student self-sufficient.* The parrot method is not conducive to such a result. As Kreisler once said, "Too much teaching can be worse than too little."

The mimicking of recordings is no less deplorable. It is far too easy today to procure the interpretive ideas of the great artists. A recording may be played over and over again until the student finally becomes unable to think of the composition except in terms of the recording artist. Such a procedure, when systematically applied, is bound to have a paralyzing effect on the musical growth of the aspiring artist. He becomes musically lazy and dependent. Neither his imagination nor his initiative are given a chance to grow, and consequently he does not develop a musical personality of his own.

A far better procedure for the serious student would be to listen to other works of the chosen composer (works that were not written for his particular instrument) and thereby acquire a feeling for the composer's over-all style and personality.

A certain qualification has to be made, however, to the above statements, owing to the fact that there are wide differences in talent among the students, not only with regard to the technical ability but also with regard to musicianship and imagination. Not every student has the potentiality of creative imagination that can develop to the point where he can become a fine performer in his own right, even when his technical abilities may be unlimited. Broadly speaking, students may be divided into an "active" and a "passive" category. The active students are those who have the innate urge of a creative imagination. They are the truly challenging ones and can be made to grow into genuine artists. The other type, the passive students, can do nothing on their own, nothing that has not been shown them by the teacher or another performer. Not even the best teacher will be able to develop something out of nothing or be able to kindle a fire where no flammable material exists. Students of the passive type will never be able to stand on their own feet musically. They will always be dependent upon a crutch— a model to imitate. They will, at best, become skillful artisans, but never real artists.

(Some students develop their musical individuality rather late in life. The teacher should patiently encourage this development. It can be very wrong to classify as hopeless a student who is slow in acquiring musical personality and imagination.)

ACOUSTICAL ELEMENTS IN PERFORMANCE: "VOWELS" AND "CONSONANTS"

Knowledge of acoustical laws is a very important element in public performance.

Anybody who talks to a few people in a small room need not raise his voice. Even if his elocution is not of the best, and even if he speaks too fast, still he will, in general, have no difficulty in making himself understood. Speaking in a large auditorium, however, to an audience of thousands is obviously an entirely different matter. The speaker will have to speak louder, slower, and more clearly. These are obvious things, yet it is strange how few are the instrumentalists who realize that the same things apply to them when they perform in public. Many do not give a thought to the fact that what is right for the drawing-room is not right for the concert hall and vice versa. In the hall the performer has to project his playing in such a manner that it will reach, in clear and understandable form, the most distant listener in the audience: he must not play just for the people in the first few rows in front, but he must perform just as much for the man at the top of the balcony. How to do this will depend largely upon the size and the acoustical properties of the hall. If the auditorium is small and the acoustics are good, not too much adjustment will have to be made. The larger the hall, the more must consideration be given to the acoustical factors. If the resonance in the auditorium is dead, then all dynamics have to be upgraded. This is easy enough in soft passages, but when the forte and fortissimo are called for the player has to have flexibility, has to know how to change his bowing when needed, dividing strokes more often, in order to get the necessary amount of sound without forcing the tone.

The nature of the accompaniment will make a great difference, too. With piano it is easier than with orchestra. If the work being performed is a heavily orchestrated concerto and if an inconsiderate conductor permits his players to drown out the soloist, the soloist is truly confronted with a practically impossible task. Whatever the circumstances may be, the performer has to have a keen ear, ready adjustment, and fast adaptability to know how delicately he may, or how robustly he must, play in order to be heard in correct balance with the accompaniment.

Speed will also be an important factor which must now be

considered a variable. Extreme speeds should better be avoided in large halls, and this is mandatory where any kind of echo effect is present in the acoustics. In such a case, too great a speed will have a tendency to blur the clarity.

To fill a hall with sound is, however, not just a matter of loudness but rather largely one of carrying power. The carrying power of a simple tone has something to do with the quality of the instrument, but still more with the quality of the tone production. The more correctly the tone is produced, the farther it will carry. On the violin the tone must not be forced.

Tone production on the stringed instruments does not consist of continuous sound only, but it has to have a certain admixture of percussive or accentuated elements, which give it character and contour.

In instrumental music, the relationship of the percussive elements to those of the purely singing sound is analogous to that of the consonants and vowels in speech and song. That consonants are essential for speech is shown by their omnipresence in every language. This same principle has to be transferred to instrumental music, where percussive sounds of a consonant character are often needed to give a clearer definition and form to the vowel sounds of the continuous tone.

On the violin, the vowel sound corresponds to the perfectly produced singing tone that has a smooth beginning and a smooth ending. The consonants (the percussive or accentuated elements) provide the articulation which can be produced by either the left or right hand. With the bow-hand, the consonant is any attack which does not have a smooth start, such as the martelé, the accented détaché, the spiccato et cetera. With the left hand, the consonant can be produced by energetic and fast dropping of the fingers for ascending passages. The counterpart, in descending passages, is a sidewise lifting of the fingers that produces almost a slight pizzicato effect. Both of these techniques, hammering of the fingers and sidewise lifting, should be applied only when that particular effect is desired.

It is very important to know well how to balance the vowels and consonants in violin playing. And in public performance one has to be mindful of the fact that the vowel-consonant balance is not the same for the concert hall as for the studio. A lesson could be learned in this respect from Chaliapin, the great Russian basso of the past. No singer ever surpassed him in the clarity of his diction. Every single word he sang could always be distinctly heard and understood by every listener in the audience. One (and perhaps the decisive) reason for this excellence became clear to me when I once heard him sing at very close range. It seemed that he was exaggerating the enunciation of the consonants. The reason for this was that he knew, by his long experience in singing in large auditoriums, that a consonant pronounced in the usual manner would not carry well enough to be heard by the distant listener.

This is a decidedly instructive example as it illustrates the necessity for carefully adjusting the consonant-vowel balance to fit the large auditorium. Applied to violin playing, the implication is that a clearer articulation is necessary in the large hall. But care must be taken not to exaggerate and to swing to the extreme, as too much "consonant" sound is infinitely more disagreeable than too much "vowel" sound, and either excess is highly undesirable.

Chapter Two
THE LEFT HAND

THE LEFT HAND IS CONCERNED with two basic problems: (1) the fingering of the notes and (2) the vibrato. All other facets of the technique have to do with the right hand and the coordination between the two hands.

BODY AND INSTRUMENT

The relationship of the instrument to the body, arms, and hands has to be one that will allow a comfortable and efficient execution of all playing movements. This is, in the last analysis, the main criterion for the "rightness" of any bodily attitude or any muscular action in connection with violin playing.

Posture

How to stand or to sit should not be the object of exact prescriptions other than that the player should feel at ease. What should be avoided are exaggerated bodily motions while playing. They are not only unpleasant to see, but they demand a constant readjustment of the bow to the violin and, therefore, add a disturbing factor to the performance.

On the other hand, it is not advisable to go to the opposite extreme, as some teachers do who insist on suppressing in their

pupils every bodily motion. There is a certain amount of movement that is natural and helps the coordination and the feeling
for rhythm and accent. Thus, bodily motion should be limited
but never completely suppressed. To determine the amount of
motion to be deleted in each case is not an easy judgment to
make, and it must be carefully and conscientiously thought
out.

In instances where a student has been drilled to a state of complete immobility it will be advisable to try to introduce, with
discretion and caution, the certain small amount of bodily movement that will help to free the student's playing from an unnatural constraint.

Holding the Instrument

Likewise, there should not be any exact rule given as to how
to hold the instrument. Some artists support the violin entirely
with the shoulder and head and are obviously comfortable doing so. Others leave the support of the instrument to the left
hand, resting the violin on the collarbone, the chin taking an
active part (pressure) on certain position shifts. For a violinist
with a long neck, the use of a pad is the most intelligent solution. (The pad should, however, be chosen from among the
types that do not touch the back of the instrument, since then
it does not absorb the tone.) One thing, however, has to be
watched: the chin must never be allowed to press on the tailpiece. This is best avoided by use of a chin-rest which straddles
the tailpiece in the middle of the instrument. Besides being more
comfortable, such a chin-rest has the further advantage of being better for the instrument, since the pressure exerted by it is
more evenly distributed.

As to the height of the scroll when the instrument is in playing position, it is better to have it higher than lower. A high
scroll throws the weight of the instrument *toward* the player's
neck and shoulder, whereas, if the scroll is too low, too much
of the weight falls toward the left hand and the bow has a tendency to slide toward the fingerboard.

Left Arm

The older schools of violin playing required every student to
pull the left elbow far to the right. Players with long arms and
fingers, who followed this rule, found that their fingers assumed
an awkward curve and leaned too heavily toward the G-string
side of the fingerboard. The wrong side of the finger tip contacted the string and more often the nail rather than the fleshy
part formed the point of contact. The immediate consequence

was the development of a severe type of handicap in all kinds of finger motion and especially in the vibrato. This illustration alone is sufficient to discredit the rule as such that the elbow should "always be placed as much to the right as possible."

The principle that correctly applies to this whole matter designates the *fingers* as the determining factor. They have to be placed in such a way as to allow them the most favorable conditions for their various actions. Once this is done, everything else—thumb, hand, arm—will subsequently find its corresponding natural position. The finger-placement will be discussed presently, but it can be said that players with short arms and fingers will have to bring the elbow fairly far to the right, whereas those with long arms and fingers will find that the elbow will remain somewhat more to the left.

The elbow, however, is never rigidly set. Whatever its basic placement, it changes its position beneath the instrument as the fingers move across the strings. When the fingers approach the G string, the elbow moves more to the right; for the E string, more to the left, except in the higher positions when it pulls to the right for all players concerned. Further, the position of the elbow will also vary to allow for different tonal results.

In the passage given in Example 1, the elbow should be placed more to the right. The run requires a crisp, percussive articulation of the fingers which is helped by moving the elbow a little to the right. Such a move results in a steeper angle in the fingers; they can hit somewhat harder and, by contacting the string with the narrower, more bony part of the tip, can produce the desired articulated sound.

In contrast, Example 2 calls for a character of softness and ease. Moving the elbow to the left will flatten the fingers by allowing them to contact the string with the bigger, softer, and fleshier pad. Keeping the fingers closer to the fingerboard will eliminate any excessive articulation. These two adjustments will produce the desired effect of smoothness.

Example 1
Lalo: *Symphonie espagnole*, Op. 21
First movement (measure 37)

Example 2
Bach: *Partita No. 2 in D Minor.*
Chaconne (measure 85)

Wrist

The wrist, too, can influence the placement of the fingers on the string. It should not allow any sideways curve in the hand, either to left or right, and should be held in such a way that there is approximately a straight alignment of the hand with the forearm, except in the half position. There are, however, further specialized exceptions. Chords involving extensions will often require the wrist to bend inward, whereas to perform certain other chords with unusual finger combinations an opposite movement of the wrist is demanded. In the higher positions the wrist will, under all circumstances, have to curve outward.

Hand

Regarding the placement of the hand, there is a school of thought that advocates that the base knuckles of the left hand should be parallel to the strings. Such a position is not natural and creates tension by the excessive turning of the hand and forearm. The hand should not remain distant from the neck of the instrument but should slightly touch both sides of the violin neck so as to help, by this easy contact, the orientation of the entire hand. The hand should not press against the instrument (should not clutch it), since this causes tensions and severely restricts the freedom of action of the fingers, hand, and arm. The contact on the side of the index finger should be maintained up to the third position. From there on upward the index finger detaches itself from the neck of the instrument. The first finger, as it falls on the string, should take the approximate shape of three sides of a square (Illustration 3, page 16).

How high (above the level of the fingerboard) or how low the hand should be set depends again upon the shape of the individual hand and fingers. The higher it is placed (the more the neck of the instrument approaches the palm of the hand) the steeper the angle of the fingers as they fall upon the strings (Illustration 7). The lower it is placed (the more the top edge of the fingerboard climbs toward the middle joint of the finger) the flatter becomes the angle of the finger-tip contact with the string (Illustration 1). This has to be carefully adjusted individually, since it affects intonation. Further discussion will follow in a moment.

Care has to be taken that the hand is not placed too far backward (toward the scroll), such as setting the hand in half position while playing in first position. Such a setting severely limits the reach of the fourth finger and places on it a constant strain. In the first position, the hand should be set in such a way that the octave B (first finger on the A string to fourth finger on the E string) falls naturally into place (Illustrations 1, 2, 3, 7, and 8). For executing, then, the F♮ on the E string or the B♭ on the A string, the first finger should be stretched backward without pushing back the whole hand (Illustrations 4 and 5).

It is safe to go even farther and to say that it is often advis-

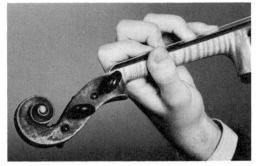

ILLUSTRATION 1 Left-hand finger place-
ments (*See also* Illustrations 2–5.)

ILLUSTRATION 2

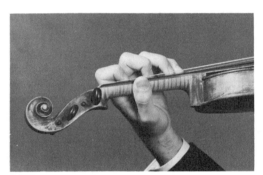

ILLUSTRATION 3

ILLUSTRATION 4

ILLUSTRATION 5

ILLUSTRATION 6 Point of contact of finger
tip on string.

able to place the hand slightly farther ahead, so that the first finger has to do a little reaching back even for the B♮, and correspondingly more so for the B♭. This actually puts the hand in a more advantageous position, since it distributes the stretch equally between the first and the fourth fingers. By positioning the hand slightly higher up the fingerboard (forward) the fingers will be given an equal extensibility in both directions, forward and backward (Illustrations 3 and 7).

Fingers and Thumb

The fingers fall perpendicularly on the tips either in the "square" position or in an elongated position, depending upon the note being played. All fingers assume the elongated shape when they reach up a half step or more from their basic placement. Illustrations 1, 2, 3, 4, and 5 show the shape of the fingers while playing different intervals in the first position. The "square" of the first two fingers is never ideally perfect. The tips of the fingers slant slightly towards the bridge and contact the strings a little to the left of the center of the finger tip (as seen from the player's viewpoint); that is, a little more of the finger tip is on the E-string side of the point of contact (Illustration 6). This left-of-center placement is specially important for the vibrato, which thereby gains in freedom and range.

The slant of the fingers should be neither too steep nor too flat, although variations of this angle will occur according to the requirements of the music, as has already been stated. A good setting of the fingers in the manner described is possible for any kind of hand, whether broad or narrow, and whether the fingers are long or short. The teacher has to analyze, in each student, what adjustments have to be made in order to permit the fingers to be placed perfectly. If the fingers are very short, then the neck of the instrument is set somewhat closer to the base knuckle, and the elbow is placed more to the right (Illustration 7). If the fingers are long, then just the opposite has to be done: the neck is closer to the middle joint and the elbow is held more to the left (Illustration 8). By means of these two variables (the position of the elbow and the vertical adjustment of the hand with regard to the neck) any hand can be positioned so that it is comfortable and can function efficiently.

The thumb needs very special attention. It is the member of the hand which is most often responsible for excessive pressure and for the clutching of the neck of the instrument. This constriction is one of the most common and most serious of faults. Clutching contributes more than anything else to the paralyzing of the functioning of the left hand.

ILLUSTRATION 7 Positioning the hand with short fingers.

ILLUSTRATION 8 Positioning the hand with long fingers.

The thumb has the function of exerting a counter-pressure against the playing fingers, and it can take care of this task most efficiently if the pressure acts from below in a direction opposed to the pressing fingers (Illustrations 2 and 7). A sidewise pressure of the thumb (on the G-string edge of the violin neck) is, for this reason, not desirable, since it does not fulfill its proper function. Such pressure also interferes severely with shifting and the vibrato.

The thumb should not stick upwards too much above the fingerboard because this position can promote the injurious sideways pressure. As always, there are exceptions: a long thumb will, of necessity, rise considerably above the level of the fingerboard, since the fingers would not otherwise be able to reach their proper places on the strings. Such hands will have to be especially guarded against the sideways pressure. Contrariwise, a short thumb will have to be placed more under the neck of the instrument. In general, the thumb should be neither completely stretched nor too bent, but rather it should approximate the curvature of the neck of the instrument.

THE MOVEMENTS OF THE LEFT HAND

Reduced to their simplest types, the movements of the left hand are as follows:

1. The vertical movements of the fingers: their dropping on and their lifting off from the strings. This is closely akin to the pianistic type of finger action, and occurs on the violin either within the normal hand position or in connection with the extensions.

2. The horizontal movement of the fingers within one position: the gliding up and down the string with a finger while the hand and thumb remain stationary. This includes simple half-step slides for the playing of accidentals within the position as well as all kinds of extensions upward or downward outside of the basic placement within the position.

3. The crossing of strings: a horizontal movement generally combined with the vertical movement of lifting the fingers off one string and setting them on another. Occasionally (for example, in certain sequences of sixths and fourths), the crossing of the string is done by a horizontal type of sliding motion without completely lifting the fingers from the fingerboard. Such a motion requires a momentary lightening of the finger pressure.

4. The sliding motion of the fingers and hand together for the changing of positions.

5. The vibrato movements: carried out either by the finger, the hand, or the arm, or by a combination of them.

Most players use too much force in all left-hand actions. They bang the fingers too hard, lift them too high, and press them too solidly after contacting the strings. To play in this manner all of the time is not only unnecessary, but also very harmful. Lifting too high slows down the action by adding to the distance that has to be covered, and the banging and pressing is apt to build tensions that are dangerous. An easy pressure, sufficient to hold down the strings, is all that is normally necessary.

Sometimes, however, a harder hitting will be in order where the music requires a certain percussiveness in passage work; or, a special accent on a single note may be called for, which can be, in a very characteristic fashion, produced by lifting the finger high and hitting it hard, resulting in what is called the "finger accent." Also, there are times when the need arises for that different tone quality that requires a greater pressure of the fingers on the strings.

The basic idea in all of this discussion is to urge the restriction of the forcefulness of the finger action to those cases where the music itself requires it. As for the rest of the time, the fingers should neither be lifted too high nor banged down too hard nor pressed excessively after contacting the string.

INTONATION

The building of good intonation rests mainly on the sense of touch in combination with the guidance of the ear. The fingers are like blind people who guide themselves through a sightless existence by touching objects which mark their paths from place to place. The analogy is pertinent to the training of the fingers on the violin. The hand learns gradually to orient itself, to find its proper location by the feel of the neck (and the body of the instrument in the upper positions). From the hand position thus secured, the fingers in their turn learn to acquire, through the sense of touch, the feeling for correct placement and for proper stretch. In this, they are continually helped, guided, and controlled by the ear.

In the shifting of positions, the process may be described as a combination of the hand finding its new location on the neck of the instrument,* of the feeling in the guiding finger for the distance covered, and of the help given by the ear as it records the progress of the shift, thereby imparting to the finger a feel for the correct distance. Eventually, this skill develops to a point where the mere act of mentally preparing the movement and thinking the sound of the desired pitch will be sufficient to cause the fingers automatically to hit the right places on the strings with accuracy. However, progressing to such an advanced stage requires help from some other factors, as we shall see, that are indispensable for acquiring a reliable intonation.

One of these factors is the setting of the *frame* of the hand, i.e., the basic placement of the fingers, first and fourth, *on the octave interval* within any one position. Functioning inside this octave frame, the second and third fingers have two positions each, one square and one extended. For example, in the A to A octave in first position on the G and the D strings, the second finger is "square" on the B♭ and the F♮, and extended on the B♮ and the F♯; the third finger is "square" on the C and the G, and extended on the C♯ and the G♯. The octave frame should be retained in each position, with the fingers reaching their assigned spots (be it by normal placement or by extensions) without abandoning the feel for this frame. This means, also, that the hand has to remain quiet and undisturbed within one position while the fingers, functioning solely from the knuckles, reach to whatever place is required, either within or outside of the frame. The basic shape of the hand *within the frame* should stay the same as far up the fingerboard as possible, which is up to about the sixth or seventh position. Emphasis on this point is necessary in the training of the student. For the advanced player, especially in playing contemporary music, the hand may function unrestricted by the basic positions. (See pages 23–24.)

In Example 3, the first measure shows the establishment of the frame of the hand, which has to be maintained, while in the succeeding measures the first finger reaches below the frame to the G♯ and the fourth finger extends upwards to B♮. This illustrates the extension outside of the frame with the hand remaining quiescent. Attention should be paid to the slightly forward position of the hand in this example, as discussed on pages 15 and 17.

The following study is excellent practice for the establishment of the frame and its maintenance during the use of the extensions. First take the key of C, and play throughout the

Example 3
Brahms: *Concerto in D major,* Op 77.
First movement (measures 482–85)

---

* The muscular action involved in the hand finding its new position is centered in the contracting or extending of the angle in the elbow, plus the drawing in or reaching outward of the arm itself. The bending of the hand in the wrist at times supplements, at other times replaces, this motion.

seven positions. Then change the signature. As a matter of course, the fundamental hand position has to remain the same or the whole purpose of the exercise will be missed (Example 4).

Example 4

Another very important intonation factor is found in the principle of the *double contact*. This was touched upon briefly in the discussion of the setting of the hand (page 15). The term signifies that the left hand has to have two points of contact with the instrument in order to orient itself properly and securely. One point, as a rule, is not sufficient. The actual points of contact will differ in various positions, as will be explained in the following paragraphs.

If, as some schools advocate, the hand is held permanently away from the violin neck so that only the thumb touches, then the hand has no secure way of establishing its location within the position or of guiding the distance during a shift. Finger action is also weakened by such placing.

In the lower positions, the double contact is provided by the thumb and the side of the first finger, each touching its corresponding side of the neck of the instrument. The contact need not be permanent or continuous in character, but it is sufficient if it occurs from time to time for the orientation of the hand. It must be very slight, since the more gentle it is, the more sensitive becomes the feeling of touching. (A blind man who contacts an object in order to orient himself will never grasp or clutch it, but instead will touch it only gently.) Any firm clutching of the left hand is a severe impediment to technical facility.

An exception to the principle of the double contact will apply in the playing of expressive passages. In order to facilitate the vibrato action, the hand can release the double contact, retaining only that of the thumb.

From the fourth position upward, the hand itself contacts the body of the violin and, thus, replaces the index finger in forming the second point of contact. Here, the side of the index finger can and ought to be separated from the instrument, because a triple contact is not useful. The triple contact does not add to the orientation and it is apt to immobilize the hand too much, especially in vibrato.

From the fifth position on, the thumb and hand contact various parts of the instrument, but the principle of double contact is still maintained. This is true even in the case of a hand with

*The fourth finger is held down silently during the playing of the second and third fingers.

a very short thumb, which requires that the thumb (for fingering in the very highest positions) leave the neck of the violin entirely and extend itself instead along the right side rim of the instrument: there is still a double contact with the thumb and the lower part of the hand.

The double contact is very helpful in finding the right place for the fingers and hand on the fingerboard.

Lastly, in this discussion of intonation, it is necessary to consider what type of intonation ought to be used: the "tempered" or the "natural." This is not the place to go into the technicalities of the two systems. No violinist can play according to a mathematical formula; he can only follow the judgment of his own ear. Be this as it may, *no one system of intonation will suffice alone*. A performer has constantly to adjust his intonation to match his accompanying medium.

The artist must be extremely sensitive and should have the ability to make instantaneous adjustments in his intonation. (The best and easiest way to make such adjustments is by means of the vibrato.) An intonation adjustable to the needs of the moment is the only safe answer to the big question of playing in tune.

The most important part in all of this is assigned, obviously, to the ear, which has to catch immediately the slightest discrepancy between the pitch desired and the pitch produced and then demand an instant reaction from the fingers.

Advanced players, already in possession of a secure intonation, will find that their facility for quick adjustment can be improved further by changing from time to time the instruments they use. It is also good advice not to interrupt the practice every few minutes to retune the violin. One should be able to play *in tune* on a violin which is *out of tune*. The performer who has acquired such a skill will never be shaken out of his assurance and authority in public performance by a recalcitrant string.

Summing up, then, these are the main factors in the building of a sound intonation: (a) a sense of touch, highly developed for the feeling of location as well as of distance; (b) constant guidance and intense control by the ear; (c) correct and facile application of the frame (the basic shape of the hand as it plays the octave interval); and finally, (d) the ability to make instantaneous adjustments in pitch to meet the musical requirements of the moment.

TIMING

The second essential factor in the development of the left hand I have called "timing." A necessary differentiation must be made between what might be called *musical timing* and *technical timing*. Musical timing means the actual sounding of the notes in the exact rhythmical pattern and the exact speed required by the music. Technical timing means the making of the necessary movements of both left and right hands at the exact moment and precise speed that will insure correct musical timing. These two things, musical timing and technical timing, will sometimes but not always coincide. In the left hand the fingers often have to be prepared ahead of the time of sounding. The same is true of the bow, which has to be placed in preparation, as in martelé or staccato bowings, before the actual playing of the notes. The musical timing is, of course, the deciding factor. If it is to be perfect, it presupposes correct technical timing of each hand by itself and a correct coordination between the two for any rhythm, any speed, or any required change of speed.

Control of timing in slow passages, or in changes of tempo, is often more difficult than the spectacular virtuoso speeds. It is an undeniable fact that even excellent violinists at times speed up or slow down not because of musical considerations but because of technical problems involved. This indicates a certain deficiency in interpretive technique which has to include the complete mastery of the timing factor. The artist's interpretive ideas should not be forced to make concessions to his technical shortcomings, and it need hardly be stressed that for any difficult passage in a piece there should be complete continuity of rhythm and tempo unless otherwise indicated by the composer. As for quality of sound in general, the difficult passages should sound as good as the easier parts and should be played so as to form an integral part of the whole composition.

The mastery of the entire timing complex (the technical timing plus the coordination of the two hands) is entirely a question of *correlation*, of the immediate and accurate response of the muscles to the directives of the mind. The reader is referred to the examples for the development of correlation which are to be found in Chapter Four (On Practicing), and he is reminded that *their importance cannot be overemphasized*.

SPECIAL TECHNICAL PROBLEMS

Shifting

There are two main categories of shifts; they will be termed the *complete shift* and the *half shift*. In the complete shift, both the hand and the thumb move into the new position. In the half shift, the thumb does not change its place of contact with the neck of the violin. Instead it remains anchored, and by bending

Example 5
Brahms: *Concerto in D major,* Op. 77
First movement (measures 338–39)

and stretching permits the hand and fingers to move up or down into other positions. This type of motion, the half shift, can be used in many instances where the fingers have to move into another position for a few notes only. Properly applied, it can greatly promote facility and security in passages that would otherwise be very cumbersome. Example 5 illustrates the point. At the asterisk, the third position is established, and the thumb then retains this point of contact, bending for the descent of the fingers into the first position, stretching for the return into the third position.

In the following pages, when speaking of "shifts" without further qualification, it is always the complete shift that is meant.

The shift is an action of the entire arm and hand, including all of the fingers and the thumb. The flexibility of the thumb, important for all facets of the left hand technique, is nowhere more essential than in shifting.

In performing the shift from the lower positions to the higher positions, the thumb moves simultaneously with the hand and the fingers. As was pointed out before, the shape of the hand in moving up the fingerboard should remain basically the same, at least up to about the sixth or seventh position. The frame of the hand, however, will become gradually smaller as the string length shortens. The span of the frame of the eighth position will be half the size of that of the first position.

In making this shift from the lower to the higher positions, the thumb will gradually pass under the neck of the instrument as the hand glides through the third and fourth positions into the higher positions. This brings the elbow rather around the violin to the right. All of this should be done in one smooth movement. In the very high positions, above the seventh, the fingers can reach easily into several positions without actually shifting the hand. For the extremely high positions, if the player's thumb is short, he may have to let it come out from underneath the neck of the violin and find a comfortable place on the rib of the instrument. In this latter case, the head will have to hold the instrument very firmly.

In moving from third to first position, the thumb should slightly precede the hand. In a move from fifth position straight down to first, the same principle applies. But if the shift is from a higher position to the third, then it is often better to make use, at least partially, of the half-shift technique: keep the thumb in place while finger and hand shift down, and then, after the shift of the hand is completed, let the thumb replace itself in the new position. The thumb thus acts as a pivot and bends during the shift but does not relinquish its contact until after the shift is completed. How soon after the shift the thumb readjusts itself will depend upon the character of the passage and especially upon the speed of the note sequence. In very fast shifts the move is almost simultaneous.

In a descending scale from the highest notes on the E string down to the first position, a player with a thumb of average length will have the ball of the thumb, at the outset, contacting the curve of the neck where it turns to join the body of the instrument. As the scale begins to descend, the thumb will exercise a slight pressure and, acting as a pivot, will pull the hand back until about the fifth position. In doing so, the thumb, which is stretched at first, gradually bends. For the further shift to about the third or fourth position the thumb still remains in place, bending a little farther and letting the hand precede, half-shift fashion. As soon as the hand completes the shift thus far, the thumb readjusts by stretching backward. It has to do so in order to be in time for the *leading* of the shift by slightly preceding the hand in the continued downward movement to first position.

A hand with a short thumb will not be able to handle long shifts in this way. The short thumb will sooner reach its comfortable limit of bending and will therefore have to readjust more often.

A descent by a big skip from the highest to the first or second position has to be done in one single, continuous arm movement, the arm gliding ahead of the hand and pulling the hand with it.

Finger pressure for the shift should be at a minimum, especially in fast passages.

There are three fundamental types of shifts:

(1) The same finger plays the note preceding and the note following the shift (Example 6).

(2) The shift (sliding motion) is performed by the finger that is on the string when the shift starts, but a new finger plays the arrival note (Example 7).

(3) The shift is performed by the finger that will play the arrival note (Example 8).

A shift that crosses strings will also fall under one of these headings as far as the left hand is concerned. (Special problems arising with double stops will be discussed in the next section.)

(4) A much-used type of shift today might be called the *retarded shift*. The finger is first stretched to a new note outside of the position in which the hand is resting at the moment, and after the stretched finger is placed on the string, the hand follows thereafter into the new position (Example 9).

Illustrations 9, 10, 11, and 12 depict this process (see next page). In Illustration 9, the stretch upward of the fourth finger from third position is shown. Illustration 10 shows the readjustment of the hand thereafter into the fourth position. The fourth finger has acted as a pivot for the hand.

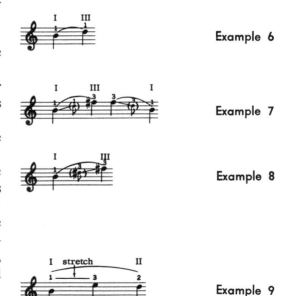

Example 6

Example 7

Example 8

Example 9

ILLUSTRATION 9 Extension of fourth finger upward.

ILLUSTRATION 10 Subsquent adjustment of the hand upward.

Illustration 11 shows the stretch backward of the first finger, preparing the hand for the downward shift from fourth position to third. The readjustment of the hand after the placing of the first finger is shown in Illustration 12.

The speed of execution of the shifting motion should be proportional to the general tempo of the passage. In slow tempos the shift is made slower; in fast tempos, more rapidly. The execution of the shift is largely a matter of timing, not only as far as the speed is concerned, but also with regard to the exact moments at which the shift is to start and to end. One of the commonest faults found in shifting is that of shortening the note preceding the move. The reason behind this fault is always a psychological one. The player worries about the shift to the point that he loses rhythmic control and nervously anticipates

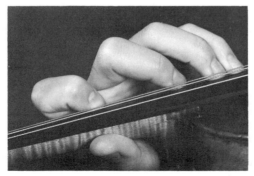

ILLUSTRATION 11 Extension of the first finger downward.

ILLUSTRATION 12 Subsequent adjustment of the hand downward.

the correct moment for the move. This gives a feeling of insecurity and great unevenness to the passage. Conscious attention to the rhythmic value and sound of the note preceding the shift is imperative until correct habits are formed.

The role of the ear is of the greatest importance for the successful performance of any shift. By listening intently before the shift and by hearing, during the shift, the gradual approach to the new pitch, the ear most effectively supplements and supports the feeling of distance provided by the sense of touch.

The bow, too, has a considerable role to play in the execution of good shifts. By moving slower and by diminishing the pressure during the actual change of position, it can eliminate a great amount of the sliding sound. This is a point that should be stressed, especially in the beginning stages of instruction. Many young students spoil an otherwise good shift by letting the bow increase in speed, or by adding bow pressure, while the left hand is in motion.

When the shift is not just a technical function necessary for the changing of positions, but is used instead as a means of expression, then, as a "glissando" or "portamento," its execution will differ. The bow will not lighten its pressure, and the movement of the finger will be slowed according to the expression desired. Also, a different type of shift will often be applied. For the sake of an expressive glissando, the shift in Example 10, for instance, can be made in three different ways. Either (a) by shifting with the first finger (type 2 shift) and then dropping the third finger (this can be called the "overslide" and is the style favored by the French school); or (b) the slide can be made by the third finger itself, which thus glides from below the note (called the "underslide" and favored by the Russian school); or finally (c) the two can be combined, the slide starting with the first finger and finishing with the third, which takes over somewhere en route.

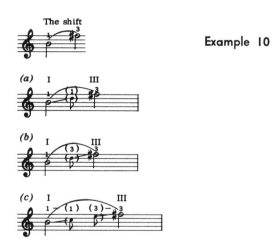

Example 10

Double Stops

Double stops present a problem for the right as well as for the left hand and will therefore be dealt with both here and in the next chapter. As far as the left hand is concerned, one of the main problems arises from the fact that with two fingers necessarily holding down two strings the danger of using excessive pressure and of building undue tension becomes acute. When two fingers grip too hard, the unnecessary tension easily spreads to the thumb and thereafter to the whole hand. The student must be cautioned never to overpress in double stops if he is to avoid stiffness and cramping of the hand.

Regarding intonation, special attention should be given to the close position of the fingers in intervals such as minor sixths or augmented fourths, which technically become half steps as far as the left hand is concerned. To treat such intervals after the manner of half steps will help greatly in perfecting their correct intonation. In scale passages of sixths or fourths, the fingers that have to cross strings from one note to the next should do so by sliding over with all pressure released but without being lifted. Much more smoothness and speed can be achieved in this manner.

In the playing of perfect fifths, the note that is too flat in pitch may be raised by leaning the finger more heavily upon that string. This is done best by turning slightly the finger and wrist and moving the elbow more to the right or more to the left as the case may be.

Octaves are most important in practicing, because they give the hand its *frame*, its basic shape. It is a good practice routine to play a scale with both fingers placed but sounding only one note; first the lower throughout, then the upper. (The same way of practicing can be applied to any kind of double stops.) In playing octaves as double stops, it is advisable to listen carefully to the lower note, since the ear is naturally quicker to hear the upper one and must be trained to hear the lower. One should not, however, make a habit of playing the lower note louder in order to hear it better. The extra bow pressure that would, in this manner, be put on the lower string can affect the pitch and would therefore require a special adjustment in the fingering.

In the playing of fingered octaves it is important to place the hand higher so that the first and second fingers reach back a little as the third and fourth stretch forward.

This same idea applies to tenths: it is best to place the hand in an intermediate position between the first and fourth fingers so that the hand can utilize its stretch in both directions, fourth finger upward and first finger downward, with no undue strain placed on either. The way in which the hand is placed in a central position is indicated in Example 11, which, by the way, is an excellent practice method for the development of tenths.

A difficulty frequently encountered in double stops is the failure of the fingers to articulate both notes of the double stop exactly at the same moment. The best way to deal with this problem is indicated in Example 12. A rhythmic variant that will shorten the troublesome notes will help most effectively in practicing.

As to shifting in double stops, the principles are fundamentally the same as in single notes.

Example 11

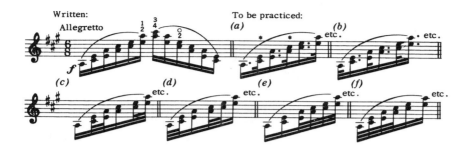

*The quick action required of the fingers in this rhythmic variation will tend to make the fingers act simultaneously.

Example 12

Jacob Dont: *24 Etudes and Caprices*, Op. 35
No. 21 (measures 1–2)

In cases where undue tension exists and where the shift thereby becomes too cumbersome (as might happen in Example 13), the student should practice lifting off the first and third fingers (after having placed the second and fourth) just before starting the shift. The shift will then begin with the second and fourth fingers, and the first and third will quickly substitute themselves for the second-fourth combination. By relaxing the first and third fingers momentarily, in the manner suggested, the hand will be helped in gradually developing a relaxed feeling throughout the passage, and the heavy sliding will be eliminated. When this easier way of playing becomes established, the first and third fingers need no longer be raised before shifting. The same formula is even more important in practicing the fingered octaves.

Example 13

When the shift is combined with a crossing of the strings, there is always one finger that acts as a pivot or *leading* finger. In Example 14, it is the third finger which connects the two double stops. It starts moving up on the A string *toward* F♯. It does not, however, glide all the way up to the F♯ but is replaced en route by the second finger as the latter approaches its note, E.

Example 14

In a shift from the lower to the higher strings, the same idea applies. In Example 15, the second finger is the pivot. At the moment the shift starts, the fourth finger lifts off, and the second finger, by gliding downward to C♯, leads the hand into the first position. During the extremely short interval of the shift, the bow is contacting only the A string.

Example 15

The playing of chords will be dealt with in some detail in the chapter on bowing. For the left hand, problems in chord playing arise especially when the chords follow each other in quick succession. This requires great agility in the fingers, since often several fingers (sometimes all four of them) have to move simultaneously from one place to another. To acquire the necessary skill, rhythmic studies, as outlined in Example 16, will be of great service as a practice device. The physical feel of the chord combination should precede the actual playing of the

(a)

long   short long   short long   short
(Also reverse the order using short long.)

(b)   etc.(c)   etc.

Example 16

Dont: *24 Etudes and Caprices*, Op. 35
No. 1 (measures 36–38)

chord. In fast successions of a number of chords, the fingers should physically anticipate as many chords ahead as possible.

For certain chords the shape of the hand and the position of the thumb have to change. For instance, in the chords quoted in Example 17, the arm and wrist must be turned inward toward the neck of the instrument for the first chord and outward for the second chord.

Example 17

Trills

The principle that fingers should *not* be lifted high and should *not* strike hard is particularly true in its application to trills. When this principle is disregarded, then the building of tension and the slowing of the performance of the trill are the inevitable results. The trill should be light in execution, the fingers having a feeling of relaxed articulation, and the trilling finger should be kept close to the string. *Over-development of strength in the fingers is especially detrimental in executing the trill.*

It is necessary to realize that the lifting of the finger in the trill is as important as the dropping of it. In fact, the trill does not begin to form as such until the finger comes *off* the string.

Very often too much attention is paid to the *beginning of a short trill*, whereas it is the *ending* that requires special care: here a slight motion of pizzicato with the trilling finger will serve well to terminate the trill with clarity and crispness. This technique can be developed by using a study such as the Dont, Op. 35, No. 6. A few lines of it are practiced with the left hand pizzicato as indicated in Example 18.

Example 18

Dont: *24 Etudes and Caprices*, Op. 35 No. 6 (adapted from measures 1–2)

Left Hand Pizzicato

In the playing of the left hand pizzicato, the string is pinched, with one of the fingers of the left hand. The elbow should be moved somewhat to the left so that more of the fleshy finger tip contacts the string and the plucking can take place in a more downward direction. The finger holding down the note that is to be sounded by the plucking finger has to be firmly set, or else the sound will be unsatisfactory.

Harmonics

Harmonics are as much a bowing problem as a left hand problem. Regarding the left hand, the fingers have to be placed exactly. For the artificial harmonics there must be a decidedly different feeling of pressure between the solidly-placed lower finger and the slightly-touching upper finger.

The double harmonic presents a special problem. Not only should the fingers be set very precisely, but also the bow should have a clear and even pressure. Sometimes one of the harmonic notes will change pitch because of the unevenness of the bow pressure. Generally speaking, it is possible to play out of tune because of wrong and uneven bow pressure.

The Chromatic Glissando

The chromatic glissando of the left hand is very similar in technique to the staccato of the right hand and should be practiced in much the same way. The finger making the glissando should be in rather a stretched (elongated) position. The wrist should be curved outward toward the scroll, the hand and arm rather tense, and the finger pressure solid. For the long glissando downward, the player's chin has to take a firm grip on the instrument. The thumb extends backward along the neck of the instrument and a staccato motion is made with the left hand while the hand and arm move simultaneously downward from the higher to the lower positions. During this whole movement, the finger should not lose its elongated shape nor the wrist its outward bend until the lower positions are reached.

The best way of practicing the long glissando is by small sections (four to six or eight notes) in tempo, to get the *driving* feel of the hand. The thumb is placed so that it pulls the hand back for the allotted number of notes; then a break is made, the thumb re-sets itself, and the next section of the run is performed. It is best if each section is done several times before progressing to the next one. Lastly, as the sections are mastered, the whole glissando is played without pause. For the glissando from the lower to the higher positions, the same routines, in reverse direction, are to be followed, the thumb remaining somewhat more passive.

FINGERINGS

There are two aspects to fingering: the musical and the technical. Musically, the fingering should assure the best sound and finest expression of the phrase; technically, it should make the passage as easy and as comfortable as possible. The two are not always in agreement with each other, and when they are at odds it is imperative that the musical purpose not be sacrificed to comfort. Always, expression has to come first and comfort second. This important principle is often disregarded, especially by certain of the modern pedagogues (and editors) who display a considerable amount of ingenuity in devising fingerings that lie well in the hand, but that are deficient with regard to sound and expression.

In the field of fingering there have been several developments that have helped to advance the left hand technique such as: (a) more playing in the even-numbered positions, (b) the half-step shift, (c) position changes on open strings, (d) better chromatic fingerings, (e) new types of extensions outside of the frame, and, finally, (f) a new kind of fingering that is based on extensions or contractions, plus the subsequent necessary readjustment of the hand itself. This last can be called the *creeping* fingering. A few words must be said concerning each of these categories.

In the older schools of violin playing, a definite preference was given throughout to the first, third, fifth, and seventh positions whereas the second, fourth, and sixth were studiously avoided. This tradition was so deeply entrenched that it took a very long time to disestablish it. Gradually the discrimination against the even-numbered positions has disappeared, and they are now placed on an equal footing with the previously favored ones. To give an example would hardly be necessary.

A shift by a whole tone (with one finger) can not be made so that it is entirely unnoticeable, and, therefore, it will always add to a passage a certain amount of sliding that might be musically undesirable. If, instead, a half-step interval is used for the change of position, then the sound of shifting can be practically eliminated. Unless the tempo of the passage is very slow, this type of shift is performed by a sudden motion of the finger, which should be made to sound as nearly as possible like the articulation of another finger dropping on the string. In modern editions examples are plentiful. (See Example 29, page 35.)

General clarity can be improved further in two ways: first, fingering the passage so that the same finger is not used on two consecutive notes (shown in the first measure of Example 19); second, changing the positions while an open string is being played, as illustrated by the second measure of the quoted passage.

Example 19
Bach: *Partita No. 1 in B Minor*
Second double (measures 4–3 from end)

Example 20

The chromatic fingering of the older schools is awkward to play and is unsatisfactory in sound, because it uses too many slides (Example 20).

The modern fingering is both easier and better in sound. It uses the half-shift technique: the thumb stays in place while the finger shifts from half to second position as shown in Example 21.

For going up and down on one string, chromatically, the traditional 1-2, 1-2 sequence is now almost entirely replaced by the 1-2-3 or 1-2-3-4. See Example 22.

The application of this new principle is shown in two illustrations from the literature (Examples 23 and 24).

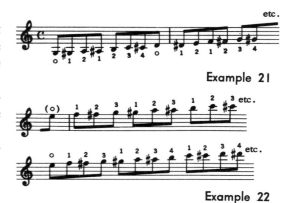

Example 21

Example 22

Example 23
Wieniawski: *Concerto in D minor*, Op. 22
First movement (measures 137–38)

Example 24
Tchaikovsky: *Concerto in D major*, Op. 35
Finale (measure 295)

Extensions outside the frame have always been a part of the violinistic equipment, but in recent times many novel types of extensions have been added, and, in general, their use has become more frequent as well as more varied. To the old type of extension belong, for example, the reaching up of the fourth finger to play C on the E string in the first position or the reaching back of the first finger to play G♯ on the E string in the third position. Double extension of two fingers at the same time was known to the older schools mostly in the form of tenths. Characteristic of the modern type of fingering are double and multiple extensions in many other forms. (These are illustrated later in this chapter.) Such extensions will often be introduced in spite of the fact that they could well be replaced by a shift. The extensions in such cases are preferred either because they make for smoother technical functioning or for a better musical effect (such as the elimination of slides with a correspondingly clearer articulation of the passage) (Example 25).

Example 25
Mendelssohn: *Concerto in E minor*, Op. 64
First movement (measures 48–43 from end)

This fingering eliminates the continuous slides that are unavoidable with the traditional fingering.

In customary fashion this modern type of extension is put to use in the *creeping* fingering. This is a change-of-position technique which eliminates the shift and is based on extensions— occasionally on contractions—*followed by a readjustment of the hand*. Whereas in the common extensions the hand does not move and the finger that makes the extension returns again to the frame, in the creeping fingering the finger places itself by stretching (or contracting) and then acts as a pivot for the establishment of a new hand position, a new frame. The hand follows the finger into the new position by a caterpillar-like crawling motion of adjustment (Example 27). Illustrations 9 and 11 show the preparation of the stretched finger prior to the readjustment of the hand (page 26). Illustrations 10 and 12 show the hand after the readjustment to the new position has been accomplished.

The appropriate technique can be developed by practicing exercises like those given in Example 26. Attention must be given to see that the pivot finger actually pulls the hand up (or down) and, in the process of doing so, changes its shape from elongated to square, or vice versa, according to circumstances, as shown in the illustrations.

Example 26(a)

* Extended finger. Hand adjusts to the new position on the following note.

Example 26(b)

† Fourth finger is placed in tune by stretching. Hand adjusts to the new position while the fourth finger is sounding.

‡ First finger is placed on its note by stretching. As first is sounding, the hand readjusts into the lower position.

With this type of fingering it is possible to cover a substantial section of any one string without audible shifting. The following examples illustrate the practical application of this method in producing a clearer and cleaner articulation.

Example 27
Beethoven: *Concerto in D. major,* Op. 61
First movement (measures 4–7 of the solo)

Example 28
Beethoven: *Concerto in D. major,* Op. 61
First movement (measures 304–306)

* Half-step shifts.
† Extension.
‡ Contraction.

Example 29
Brahms: *Concerto in D major,* Op. 77
First movement (measures 252–55)

In Example 27, two fingerings are given, one above the notes and the other below. In Example 29 the asterisks show the shift by a half-step slide, the dagger shows the extension of the fourth finger, after which the hand readjusts itself into the fourth position, and the double daggers show the downward contraction-creeping.

The new devices for the elimination of slides have led many violinists to the extreme of trying to avoid all slides. To do so deprives violin playing of a great deal of color and makes it dry and cold. The right idea is to do away with slides that are musically undesirable, but, by all means, not to cast out the good with the bad by eliminating also those glissando slides that are musically justified.

The use of fingering for coloring purposes has been known for a long time. The choice of a fingering to allow for an expressive glissando or the substitution of the third for the fourth finger for the sake of a better vibrato quality and richer sound

Example 30
Vieuxtemps: *Grand Concerto in D minor,* Op. 31
First movement (measure 39 of the solo)

* Finger accent.

Example 31
Wieniawski: *Concerto in D minor,* Op. 22
First movement (measure 144)

Example 32
Franck: *Sonata in A major for piano and violin*
First movement (measure 99)

Copyrighted 1915 by G. Schirmer, Inc. Used by permission.

Example 33
Bruch: *Concerto in G minor,* Op. 26
First movement (measures 36–37)

Example 34
Bach: *Sonata No. 3 in C major*
First movement: Prelude (measure 20)

are well known, and there is no need to amplify here. The "finger accent" (that particular emphasis produced by the lifting and hard hitting of a finger) has been mentioned previously. Such an accent is most effective when followed by an intense vibrato. A good illustration of its proper use is shown in Example 30.

The *substitution of fingers* is a very valuable fingering device. It can help the technical execution of a passage and/or its expressiveness. Where, in a slurred legato phrase, a note is repeated, the substitution must be made (Examples 31 and 32).

On the expressive side, the substitution can be used effectively in a succession of notes to change the character of the sound and the intensity of the vibrato (Example 33).

In Example 34, from the Bach C major Prelude, the substitution technique of shifting alternately from the second to the third finger and from the third to the second greatly facilitates the execution of this very troublesome measure.

Contrary to the professed convictions of most pedagogues, I most emphatically believe in varying the fingerings, in changing them from time to time. Scales, arpeggios, and other similar studies should be worked with different fingerings, as will be explained later in some detail; and when pieces that have been played before are taken up again, some of the fingerings may be altered. This keeps a piece from getting stale and frozen, stimulates the imagination, and gives a new freshness of approach. Nothing is worse in violin playing than becoming a slave either to tradition or to habit and of being bogged down, thereby, in a sort of musical rut. Sticking rigidly to the same fingerings is one of the ruts that make for inflexibility in performance and prevent the playing from acquiring that quality of spontaneity and near-improvisation that is so eminently desirable. It is, of course, not a question of fingering alone but rather a question of the whole attitude toward playing and performing. Fingering is one factor, by no means a negligible one; and I do feel that by acquiring (through building a facility in changing fingerings and bowings) an independence from set patterns, a violinist's whole mental approach to playing will gain in flexibility and freedom. That a player with such facility will not be ruffled when, by accident, he takes an unplanned fingering or bowing, is another added advantage of such training.

A teacher must, of course, prescribe fingerings as long as the student is not yet far enough advanced to choose his own. These must be in good taste and technically practical. The thoroughly proficient student should definitely be encouraged in independence and in his own personal variations in fingering. His whole style of playing will profit thereby.

VIBRATO

Types of Vibrato

The schools are, at present, divided on the question of what is the right form of vibrato. Should it be performed by the arm, the hand, or the fingers? Each of these three types has its characteristics, and I feel that because of their different color possibilities all three should be developed and used. The variety resulting from the combination of these three types gives the performer a far wider range of coloring and expressiveness and a more personal tone quality.

Although these three types can be fairly well isolated for practice purposes, it is only very rarely that a pure form of any one of them will be found in artistic performance. The developed vibrato may be centered either in the arm, the hand, or the finger, and that particular type will then predominate, but, if there is no stiffness to prevent it, each vibrato type will normally bring about an interplay of the neighboring muscles and therewith introduce elements of the other two types.

Within each of these three types, speed, width, and intensity can be varied to a fairly great extent, with the exception of a somewhat limited width in the finger vibrato. The player should be capable of controlling speed, width, and intensity within each type; of slowing, speeding up, or stopping the vibrato at will; of making the motion wider or narrower; or of changing the pressure of the finger and its angle with the string. He should be capable of changing from one type of vibrato to another in gradual transition with subtlety and smoothness so that no line of demarcation will be apparent. Moreover, he should be able to mix the various types. This is what is implied by perfect vibrato control. A player thus equipped is in a position to color his tone exactly as he feels it ought to be colored in any particular instance. This may sound somewhat artificial on paper, but once the vibrato is truly mastered in all of its aspects, the practical control becomes subconscious and spontaneous—from the "white" sound of no vibrato to that of the greatest intensity.

In general, the vibrato will have to be adapted to the dynamics of the bow, becoming more intense and wider in forte, more subdued, narrower, and less fast in piano. The arm vibrato is the most intense and the finger vibrato the gentlest. Strong dynamics will be more likely to bring the arm into action; soft passages will be limited to finger and hand. But there are exceptions: some soft passages require a very intense and fast type of vibrato, and quite often the most forceful dynamics can be dealt with by the hand vibrato.

Although we will find that a wide vibrato is usually slower and a narrow one faster, the player has to be able to combine wide with fast as well as narrow with slow, because these combinations provide different shadings which are sometimes needed.

The vibrato coloring is, fundamentally, a matter of personal taste, but this personal taste must never lose sight of the requirements of musical style. Mozart will obviously call for a different coloring from Brahms. In Mozart, the vibrato will have to be narrower and combined with extreme clarity of tone. In Brahms, the vibrato will, for the most part, be wider and the tone production broader. Similar adjustments have to be made to fit the particular style of each composer and of each composition.

The combining of all of the types of vibrato with all of the dynamic nuances and shadings of which the bow is capable can result in an endless succession of possibilities for giving life, color, and variety to a violinist's performance.

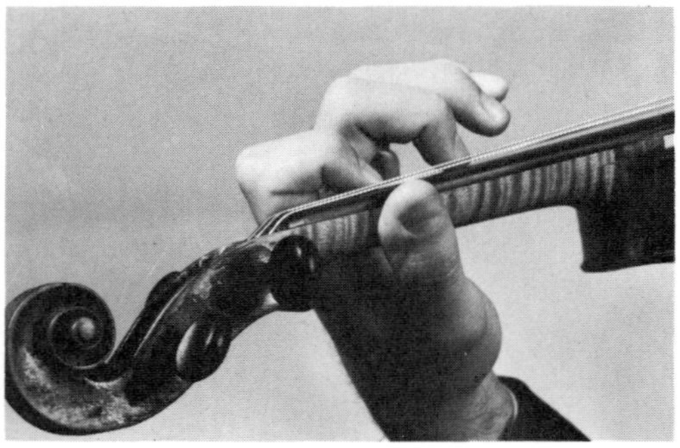

The Study of the Vibrato

One thing has to be emphasized at the beginning, since it applies to all forms of the vibrato with equal force: the hand must, under no circumstances, squeeze the neck of the instrument. Attempting to vibrate while squeezing will create an intense strain and paralyze any action of the hand. Almost all beginners will squeeze when they start out to learn the vibrato, because they feel that it is something very difficult and their psychological reaction is to hold on tightly. The first thing the teacher has to do is to loosen the student's hand in its grip of the neck and then to check constantly to see that it remains flexible.

THE HAND VIBRATO. In this type of vibrato, the hand swings from a more-or-less immobilized arm. For this reason it is often referred to as the "wrist vibrato." * The finger elongates itself as the hand swings backward toward the scroll and then resumes its original curved position as the hand returns to its starting point. See Illustrations 13 and 14.

To practice this vibrato the hand is best placed in the third position with the lower part of the hand contacting the body of

ILLUSTRATION 13 Starting position for the vibrato: squared fingers.

ILLUSTRATION 14 Backward swing in the vibrato: flattened fingers.

---

* The terminology "wrist vibrato" is not accurate. It is as wrong to call the hand vibrato wrist vibrato, as it would be to term the arm vibrato, "elbow vibrato."

the instrument (Illustration 15). The second finger is placed in tune on the A string (E♮), and the hand drops backward from the wrist and returns forward to its starting position. The finger submits to the motion by stretching and must not lose its place on the string by allowing itself to be pulled backward by the hand. The finger itself describes on the string a rocking motion whereby its point of contact changes from a place closer to the nail to one farther back on the finger tip. With this motion the pitch changes from the initial E slightly toward the flatted side. As the hand returns to the starting position, the finger resumes its original shape and point of contact on E♮, and therewith the vibrato cycle is completed. During the learning process, the contact of the lower palm of the hand with the body of the instrument has to be maintained in order to insure the immobilization of the arm. The side of the index finger will best be detached from the neck of the instrument. For the initial steps, it is good to start with an exact number of pulses per beat: two motions, then three, four, six, then more without counting them. Rhythmic variations such as those shown in Example 35 are very useful.

Resting the scroll of the violin on the music stand or against the wall is often a helpful device in the beginning stages.

Many beginners will have difficulty with the vibrato because they start the movement with the fingers instead of with the hand. They try to make the hand (or the arm) move by elongating the finger. Instead, the impulse should come from the hand (or arm). The finger should move only passively, yielding and letting itself be moved by the actions of the hand. The best way to overcome such difficulty when it exists is for the teacher first to ease up and free completely the position of the student's hand; then to grasp the loose skin under the base knuckle of the vibrating middle finger (the second finger) and perform the vibrato swing for him. This will soon give the student the feeling for the correct movement and the passive yielding of the finger.

When the vibrato begins to function well in third position, it should then be tried in the lower positions. At the outset there may be some difficulty from the loss of hand-support on the instrument. In this case the teacher can insert two or three fingers between the lower part of the student's hand and the body of the instrument, thus giving the latter the same feeling of support he has had in the third position, and immobilizing his arm, which is not used actively in the hand vibrato (Illustration 16). As soon as his vibrato gets well under way, the teacher withdraws his own fingers. In this way the student will quickly acquire independence from the hand-support. The teacher will

ILLUSTRATION 15 Setting the hand for the initial practice of the hand (wrist) vibrato.

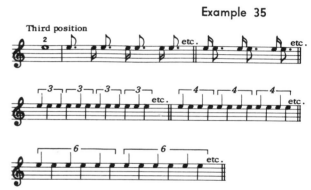

Example 35

Stems up: hand in tune, forward position.
Stems down: hand rocks backward, slight flatting of pitch.

ILLUSTRATION 16 Assisting the hand to vibrate in first position.

do well to see that there is no pressure on the neck of the instrument by the side of the first finger, when the development of the vibrato in the first position is being practiced. Transfer of the vibrato to the higher positions (above the third) will present a problem only when the hand is very high up the fingerboard. This is especially true on the G string where the elongated shape of the fingers may sometimes make the hand vibrato impractical. In such cases this type of vibrato has to be replaced by the arm vibrato.

THE ARM VIBRATO. The principles underlying the acquisition of the arm vibrato are much the same as those given for the hand vibrato. The impulse, instead of coming from the hand, now comes from the forearm, and, in this case also, the finger has to yield passively. The finger should be firm enough to hold the string down and to retain its place on the string, but flexible enough to submit to the motion of the arm. It must stretch and recurve with the backward and forward swing of the vibrato cycle. The same rhythmic methods should be applied just as described for the hand vibrato. At the beginning of the development of the arm vibrato, it is advisable to bend the wrist outward toward the scroll and to keep it locked in this position. To start in the first position will be as good as in any other position.

For starting this vibrato in positions higher than the third, it is often helpful, for practice purposes, to place the second finger on the string and to permit the hand to strike the rib of the instrument with every forward swing, as if playing a trill with the palm of the hand on the edge of the violin. This helps in acquiring evenness and rhythm in the movement.

The arm vibrato can occasionally serve a good pedagogical purpose in cases where a student has a very bad type of hand vibrato. It will often be advisable under such circumstances to stop the hand vibrato completely for a period of time and to replace it by an arm vibrato, rather than to attempt immediately to correct the faults of the former. The hand muscles will relax sooner in this manner, and when they do, the hand vibrato will almost immediately work better and more naturally.

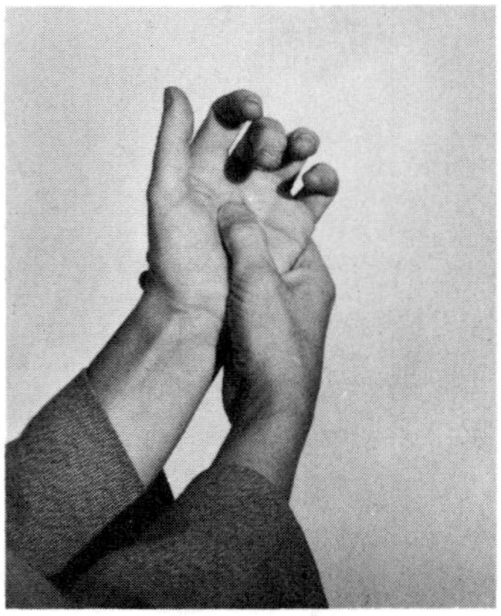

THE FINGER VIBRATO. A good finger vibrato is more difficult to acquire than are the other two types, and it should not be attempted until the hand and arm vibratos are under full control. The impulse comes from the finger itself, which swings from its base knuckle with the hand slightly yielding and moving passively in flexible response to the finger action. This vibrato is smaller in width than the other types. It can be practiced without the instrument by holding the left hand between the thumb and fingers of the right hand, as shown in Illustration 17, in

ILLUSTRATION 17 Practice position for the finger vibrato.

order to immobilize the palm of the hand; thereupon a quick, shaking motion of the fingers is executed.

THE FINGER TIP VIBRATO (simulated finger vibrato). In passages that are too fast to admit of a regular vibrato, but which should be expressive, the illusion of a vibrato can be created by flattening the fingers and letting them break slightly in their knuckles immediately after the note is sounded (Illustrations 18 and 19). The elbow is placed more to the left to flatten the fingers and the fingers themselves move in a lazy fashion, lifting but little and slowly, and dropping also slowly; after touching the string, the finger-knuckle gives in. Illustration 18 shows the finger at the very moment of contact with the string and Illustration 19 shows the breaking of the knuckle immediately thereafter.

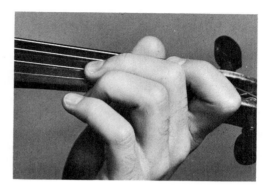

ILLUSTRATION 18 Setting the finger for the fingertip vibrato.

The foregoing discussion would not be complete without calling attention to the fact that the shape of the player's fingers has an important influence on the several types of vibrato. Those who have narrow and bony finger tips will be well advised to place the fingers on the strings using a flatter angle.

METHODS OF LOOSENING THE FINGER JOINTS. Any type of vibrato requires flexible and loose finger joints. Wherever there is a need to improve their flexibility, a good method is to place the fingers on the string and, without using the bow, alternate a stretching and a bending of the joint nearest the nail, by sliding the finger forward and backward on the string. Another method of loosening the finger joints is the substitution of lower numbered fingers for higher numbered fingers on the same note without moving either the hand or the wrist, using only finger action to accomplish the switch. Example 36 gives a sample exercise. It is to be performed throughout in any one position with the lower finger being stretched up to replace the higher finger in each case.

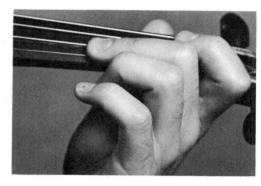

ILLUSTRATION 19 Collapsed finger in the fingertip vibrato.

Example 36

First position *throughout*

* Extensions without shifting the hand.

The playing of the chromatic scale using the sliding fingering will also help to increase the flexibility of the finger joints; and the playing of scales or other exercises with flattened fingers (after the manner shown in Illustration 19) will aid the player in acquiring the feel of the flat joint. However, such practice should be done solely for this particular purpose. Let us remind the reader that all of the aforementioned exercises should be practiced only by those who need them. The first one especially (breaking the knuckles inward) could have disastrous effects with a hand that is already too loose and weak in the finger joints.

Special Problems in the Vibrato

The foregoing discussion has dealt with the practice methods for the development of the various types of vibrato. It is necessary, however, to add a few words about the several aspects of the vibrato in general, beyond its initial stages of development.

INTONATION OF THE VIBRATO. It is important that the vibrato always go to the flatted side of the pitch. The ear catches far more readily the highest pitch sounded, and a vibrato that goes as much above pitch as below makes the general intonation sound too sharp. The finger should fall in tune on the string. The vibrato should slightly lower the pitch by swinging first backward, and then should re-establish the correct pitch by its forward swing. Whenever a distinct wavering of the pitch occurs, the reason for it may be one of the following: the vibrato is either too wide or too slow; the fingers are too weakly placed on the strings; or, there is too much sharping of the pitch by the vibrato motion itself.

DIRECTION OF THE VIBRATO MOTION. The vibrato motion does not normally occur exactly parallel to the length of the string, since this would deprive the vibrato of much of its ease as well as its range of motion. Rather, it directs itself across the string at an acute angle to the string's length.

SPEED OF THE VIBRATO. In general the vibrato may be speeded up by the simple device of reducing its width. The less distance the hand has to cover, the more vibrato cycles it can negotiate per beat. Besides, the idea of cutting down on the distance moved is less likely to produce tension in the student than is the definite focusing of the conscious effort directly on the speeding-up process. Although it is easier to attain greater speed when the width is small, one must be able also, as was said before, to vibrate wide and fast as well as narrow and slow.

One other factor must be mentioned in the speeding-up process, and that is the position of the wrist itself. If the wrist is set so that it bends slightly outward (toward the scroll), it will contribute to an increase of speed in the hand vibrato, since this tends, at the same time, to reduce the distance that can be covered.

DOUBLE STOPS WITH VIBRATO. Whenever problems occur in the vibrato on double stops, it is best to practice first one finger, then the other, with vibrato; lastly, both together. Certain chords, requiring the setting of three or more fingers, cannot be played with a wrist vibrato. In such cases, the only solution is the use of the arm vibrato.

CONTINUITY OF THE VIBRATO. There are players who have the bad habit of starting the vibrato after the note has already sounded and an appreciable length of bow has been expended upon it. This style of playing may have its place occasionally as a color factor, but it should not degenerate into a mannerism that is applied to every single note. The following exercise will help in correcting this bad habit.

1. Start a single note with an intense and sudden vibrato and then, while diminishing the sound, let the vibrato become more gentle. Repeat this on each note of the scale.

2. Next, practice long tones without diminuendo and keep the vibrato going without interruption during the change of bow stroke.

3. Finally, practice two or more notes legato (slurred) on one bow with the vibrato carrying over from one note to the next. In this exercise, the flow of the bow stroke produces a sympathetic feeling of continuity in the left-hand vibrato action.

Chapter Three
THE RIGHT HAND

WE NOW TURN OUR ATTENTION to the problems of the right hand, which generally cause most of the trouble for the violinist.

FUNDAMENTALS

The fundamentals have to do with the adapting of the natural motions of the right arm, hand and fingers to the technique of the bowing. These will be taken up under four headings: (1) the system of springs; (2) holding the bow; (3) the physical motions of the arm, hand, and fingers; and (4) the drawing of the straight stroke.

The System of Springs

To understand the functioning of the bow, one has to realize from the very outset that the whole right arm technique is based on a system of *springs*. These react in much the same way as do mechanical springs. Violinistically, they are partly artificial (such as the resilience of the bow hair and the flexibility of the bow stick) and partly natural (such as the joints of the shoulder, elbow, wrist, fingers, and thumb). If a bow were to be made whose stick and hair were entirely rigid and unyielding, it is not difficult to imagine how bad the tone and how impossible the performance of most of the varieties of bowing would be. On the other hand, given the very finest of bows, with perfect resiliency, nothing really constructive can be accomplished unless the natural springs are in working order; unless the joints of the fingers, thumb, hand, and arm are flexible and springlike. There has to be this resiliency and springiness in the functioning of the whole arm from shoulder to finger tips or else the tone will be hard and ugly, the bowing clumsy and uncontrolled.

Flexibility in the arm, hand, and fingers is as natural for their functioning as is flexibility in the legs, feet, and toes in the process of walking. There should be an appearance of ease in the bowing, and it should not resemble the stiffness that would occur if one were to try to walk without bending the proper joints.

The springs are not necessarily loose all of the time. We can, and we have to, set them at various degrees of firmness. With the bow, we do it by tightening and loosening the hair; with the natural springs, we can do it by muscular action. But even though the springs can occasionally be very firm, they must never lose their basic springlike quality by becoming actually rigid. Therefore, the bow should be held in such a way as to allow the freest play in the working of all of the springs involved, their interaction and coordination.

Holding the Bow

In describing how the bow should be held, the basic or neutral grip will be presented first. It is the bow-hand position that should be taught to beginners. However, in actual playing this position of the bow hand is not a fixed or invariable thing, but rather, as will be shown later in detail, it is subject to constant modification as the bow moves from one end to the other and as the player changes his dynamics, bowing styles, and tonal qualities.

The basic grip as given here permits the flexibility of the hand to develop rather quickly, because it is a *natural* position of the hand. This manner of holding the bow is designed chiefly to release the springs of the hand and fingers so that the bow can settle deeper into the strings. It is the best grip for the achievement of fullness and roundness of sound.

To set this basic position, take the bow in the left hand, pointing it vertically upward with the hair facing the player. With the right hand, form a circle by placing the tip of the thumb against the second * finger as shown in Illustration 20. Bring

---

* The terminology used throughout this book is "thumb," "1" (index finger), "2" (middle finger), "3" (ring finger), "4" (little finger).

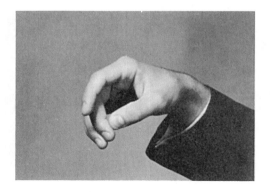

ILLUSTRATION 20 Contact point of thumb and second finger preparatory to holding the bow.

ILLUSTRATION 21   Positioning the contact point near the frog.

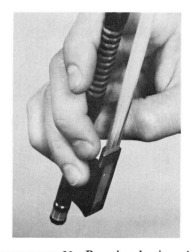

ILLUSTRATION 22   Bow hand, view A.

ILLUSTRATION 23   Bow hand, view B.

this circle over to the bow, not directly at right angles but from slightly above (Illustration 21). Open the circle a little and insert the bow-stick so that the thumb contacts the stick and the frog. (The thumb should not be placed into the cut-out of the frog, nor should it protrude on the opposite side of the stick.) In doing all of this, the thumb should retain the same position in relation to the second finger that it had in the forming of the initial circle. This means that, above all, it has to retain its easy, natural, outward curve and has to keep the inner edge of its tip turned toward the second finger as shown in Illustration 22.

The second finger will be curved over the stick opposite the thumb and will contact the stick at the joint nearest the nail. The third finger reaches over the frog (Illustration 22).

The fourth finger is placed on the stick rather close to the third finger. The section of the stick immediately above the frog is always of octagonal construction, even when the stick itself is round. In placing the fourth finger, its tip rests not directly on top of the stick, but instead on the inner side of the octagon, contacting the flat surface just next to the top. (Illustrations 23, 29, and 34 show this best.) In this position the fourth finger does not slide over the frog nor off the stick. This placement is important, because it facilitates the handling of many of the active controls in the various bowings in addition to its fundamental function of counterbalancing the weight of the bow.

The fourth finger is placed close enough to the third finger that a slight curve forms at each joint. If it is stretched too far out toward the end of the stick, the curves cannot form, and it becomes stiff and rigid, losing thereby its springlike action. This fourth finger can also become "locked" by curving too much and by being set too close to the third finger. A healthy medium has to be found, one in which the finger remains completely flexible and does not become stiff either by too much curve or by no curve at all.

The first finger is placed at a slight distance from the second finger and contacts the stick of the bow a little on the nail side of the middle joint (Illustration 23). This placement of the first finger enables the bow to get a far better hold on the strings as the attack is made, to "catch" the string as it were, on the down-bow especially; and the hand acquires more directly the feel of the resistance between bow-hair and string. When the contact with the bow is not in the right place on the finger (between middle knuckle and joint nearest the nail), the student can correct it by releasing the tip of the first finger from its contact with the stick and pushing it very slightly away from the second finger.

The four fingers on top of the bow stick should rest there with the same slight distance between them that is natural when the hand hangs loosely suspended from the wrist and completely relaxed. The single exception to this is that the first finger may be set very slightly away from the second finger.

Placed in this fashion, the fingers control a larger part of the bow and give a more secure hold on it. Placed too far apart, they can stiffen the entire hand. Placed too close together, they lessen the control and, when pressure is added, the sound will have a tendency to become strident. The worst mistake of all is to press the fingers against each other, thus creating a great deal of unnatural and useless tension.

The *correct* bow grip must be a comfortable one; all fingers are curved in a natural, relaxed way; no single joint (knuckle) is stiffened; and the correctly resulting flexibility must allow all of the natural springs in the fingers and the hand to function easily and well.

At the beginning of this section mention was made of the fact that the bow grip is subject to adjustments when various musical effects are desired. The mechanics of playing a forte and a piano dynamic, for example, are very different from each other; one should not expect that a single way of holding and manipulating the bow would be equally suited both to the production of a light, airy, and transparent sound and to the vigorous motion of the fast and broad détaché.

For the transparent sound, the first finger moves more toward its base joint in its point of contact with the stick and the other fingers come slightly off the stick (Illustration 24).

When the bow needs to settle into the string more, for breadth of sound, the position of the index finger will again be readjusted, as shown in Illustration 25. Here the wrist acquires a feeling of "pulling" the bow, and the first finger, in its slight spreading away from the middle finger, feels a closer contact with the stick and the functioning of the bow-hair on the string.

In the very broad and fast détaché, when the bow has a great speed of motion, it is generally useful to let the first finger contact the stick nearer the middle joint. This will require an adjustment in the shape of the other fingers as they rest on the stick (Illustration 26). For further discussion on applying these various bow grips, see the section on faulty tone production, pages 63–64 in this chapter.

The Physical Motions

All of the movements of the right hand are executed with the bow forming an integral part of the whole right-hand mech-

ILLUSTRATION 24 Bow hand set for the transparent sound.

ILLUSTRATION 25 Bow hand set for breadth of sound.

ILLUSTRATION 26 Bow hand set for the broad fast détaché.

ILLUSTRATION 28 Horizontal finger-motion in the bow hand: strokewise.

ILLUSTRATION 29 Pivoting finger-motion for adjusting the angle of the bow on the strings.

anism. Since the bow grip determines exactly how the bow is being integrated into this playing unit, the grip itself has to be discussed before a survey of the various movements of the finger-hand-arm entity can reasonably be presented.

An outline of the basic movements occurring in the handling of the bow follows, its purpose being to serve as an easy reference guide in the subsequent text and thereby to avoid unnecessary repetitions. The motions will be classified and described as simply as possible with neither the intention nor the pretense of giving a physiologically exact or complete account.

Before dealing individually with these classified motions, it is pertinent to call attention to the fact that all natural motions of the hand, arm, and fingers as such are circular in character. The motion of bending at any one joint causes an arc to be described by the outer extremity of the section of the arm in motion. Therefore, straight-line motion forms only through a combination of movements which are naturally circular. Further discussion will be found on pages 51 and 53.

In reading the following discussion it is a good idea to keep in mind that the finger motions are used for the smaller, more delicate adjustments and that the hand and arm come into play as the broader and less sensitive effects are desired.

MOTIONS OF THE FINGERS AS SUCH.

Vertical Motion (Illustration 27). The fingers, and thumb, in combination, can move in a way that will raise and lower the bow vertically. This motion can be delegated entirely to the fingers, with the hand having no part in it but remaining static in the wrist joint. Suspending the bow an inch above the strings, such finger action places it on the strings and lifts it off again. It should be practiced in this manner.

Horizontal Motion (Illustration 28). This is the horizontal stroke-motion. The fingers and thumb can move the bow in the lengthwise direction of the stick and can therefore execute short, regular bow strokes of their own accord. At the end of such down-bow strokes, the thumb and fourth finger will be almost entirely straightened and in reversing the motion for the up-bow, the fingers and thumb gradually resume their original curved position. One must pay particular attention to the thumb in this motion to see that it is active in the straightening and re-curving process. This movement should be practiced first in the middle of the bow, using very small strokes.

Horizontal Turning (Pivoting) Motion (Illustration 29). This motion causes the point of the bow to swing in a *horizontal* arc around the tip of the thumb as a center (upper hand in Illustration 29). With the second finger passive, this motion involves a stretching forward of the fourth finger by pushing with it at its point of contact on the stick and simultaneously pulling on the bow with the first finger. The third finger reacts with the fourth finger. The reverse motion brings the fingers back to their original position. This action varies the angle of the bow in relation to the bridge and is used in minor adjustments in the *direction* of the bow-stroke, especially in short, reiterated strokes as in the spiccato or the quick détaché.

Vertical Turning (*Pivoting*) *Motion* (Illustration 30). This is the motion that causes the bow to rotate *vertically* so that the point of the bow describes a perpendicular arc around the tip of the thumb as center. When the bow is held in the air horizontally, the vertical rotation can be achieved by alternately pressing and releasing the fourth finger. Pressure in the fourth finger will cause the tip of the bow to swing upward. Releasing the pressure will allow the weight of the bow to swing it back downward. The bow thus rocks vertically around the fulcrum of the thumb and second finger. Consequently, this type of finger action (second finger stationary, first finger moving down when the third and fourth fingers move up) can be used to control and vary the pressure applied to the strings. It has other applications as well, such as in string crossings near the frog of the bow in which this particular type of motion supplements a rotation of the hand in the wrist joint.

Lengthwise-Axis Rotation. By rolling the bow between the thumb and fingers, it can be made to rotate around its own lengthwise axis so that the stick will alternately lean toward the bridge or toward the fingerboard. This motion of the fingers is only rarely used, but it can serve to help regulate the amount of hair that contacts the string. In actual playing, however, it is more practical to achieve this type of regulation by "wrist-motion" (lowering or raising the hand in the wrist joint).

The small and subtle motions of the fingers and the thumb, as described in the preceding paragraphs, are used for many delicate controls. They are the little precision tools that are needed for the exacting and sensitive jobs as contrasted with the big tools that do the work when the larger and more robust effects are called for.

MOTIONS OF THE HAND IN THE WRIST JOINT (Illustration 31). The motions under this heading are those that are most commonly called "wrist motions." This terminology, at best, lacks precision, since the *motions* in question are actually movements of the hand *from* the wrist and not, as the terminology suggests, *of* the wrist as such. However, having made this observation, we shall not be overly pedantic about it.

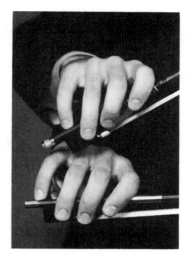

ILLUSTRATION 30 Pivoting finger-motion for vertical rotation of the point of the bow.

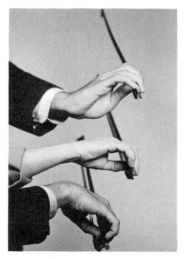

ILLUSTRATION 31 Varying the angle of the bow hand to the arm: wrist flexibility.

Vertical Movement of the Hand. The hand can swing up and down in relation to the forearm. "Up" and "down" are to be understood as motions which originate from a level position of the forearm and hand, held horizontally, palm downward, wrist flat, as shown by the middle hand in Illustration 31. The up motion of the hand forms a so-called "low" wrist, a bending in or pushing down of the wrist (upper hand in the illustration). This reverses itself when the hand drops downward, forming the "high" wrist (lowest hand in Illustration 31).

Horizontal Movement of the Hand. Again, let us suppose that the hand is held horizontally in a straight line with the forearm, palm downward. A certain amount of lateral motion is possible for the hand, in the direction of the thumb, left, and toward the fourth finger, right. This movement has a much smaller range than the up and down motion, but it is, nevertheless, highly important in many types of bowing.

These two motions can be combined so as to allow the hand to move in *any* direction, and to describe completely circular motions around the axis that runs lengthwise of the forearm.

MOTIONS OF THE FOREARM.

Open-Close Motion. The forearm can bend and straighten, hinge fashion, in the elbow joint with the effect of closing and opening the arm. This is probably the most important of all bowing movements and it is used in almost every type of bowing stroke.

Forearm Rotation. The forearm can rotate in the elbow joint around its own lengthwise axis so that it can turn the hand, without any assistance from the upper arm, from a position with the palm facing the floor to one almost directly facing the ceiling. This is the movement used so much in daily life for turning door knobs or keys in locks. Very important in bowing technique, it is a motion that is often mistaken for a hand movement. The technical terms for these turning motions are: (1) palm turning downward, *pronation;* (2) palm turning upward, *supination.*

MOTIONS OF THE UPPER ARM. The upper arm has the widest range of possible motions, but only two are useful for the bowing.

Vertical Motion of the Upper Arm. This is the motion of the upper arm which swings the elbow out away from the body and permits it to drop again close to the side. The motion is used mainly in the crossing of strings.

Horizontal Motion of the Upper Arm. This is the motion from left (front) to right (back) and return which is common to the plain bow stroke, especially when the bow is used between the frog and the middle.

A combination of these two motions can result in all varieties of oblique and curved motions, which occur in the many types of bowings. For instance, the motion that forms the horizontal bow stroke on the G string will become a mixture of the two when *crossing* to the E string.

Apart from all of these motions, which have their own legitimate places within the technique of the bow arm, one encounters often another movement, that of raising (shrugging) the shoulder. This occurs frequently as the bow approaches the frog. Such a movement *has no place at all* in a sound bowing technique. In fact, it is the evil source of frustrations and disturbances in the bow arm and, for the sake of a healthy bowing development, should be eliminated as soon as possible.

Drawing the Straight Bow Stroke

The straight bow stroke from frog to tip is the foundation of the entire bowing technique. The bow has to be drawn in a straight line, parallel to the bridge, for two good reasons. One is that a crooked bow stroke causes the bow to change promiscuously its place of contact on the string and to vary at random its distance from the bridge. The second reason is that a crooked bow stroke impairs the quality of the sound. (See also page 61.)

The chief problem in the straight bow stroke is to be found in the fact that action in the form of a straight line does not come naturally to the members of the human body. The bending of the joint causes circular motion to take place, as was said before. This being the case, a straight line can result only through the well-coordinated combination of circular motions. This fact alone explains why it is that beginners, as well as many players who are a good way past the beginning stages of study, have such great difficulty in drawing a straight bow with ease and assurance.

THE THREE STAGES OF THE STROKE: TRIANGLE, SQUARE, AND POINT. There are three distinct stages of the whole-bow stroke. (1) When the bow is set on the strings at the very frog, a triangle is formed by the arm and instrument as shown in Illustration 32. (2) When the bow is set on the string at approxi-

ILLUSTRATION 32 Setting of the bow at the frog: "triangle position."

mately the middle (the exact place varies with the individual player) a square is formed (Illustration 33). Notice that this right angle in the elbow will form *somewhere* in every bow arm. By straightening up this square (which with some players becomes more of an elongated rectangle) the player will find that his shoulder will tend to relax, his arm to hang naturally from the shoulder, and his wrist to become almost level with his arm and hand. (3) When the bow is set on the strings at the tip, the right arm is then stretched out nearly straight, the elbow's right angle now becoming almost a straight angle (Illustration 34).

The control of the bow is easiest and most natural near the square position, and it is best, therefore, to begin the study of the bow stroke at the square and to work from there toward the point and the frog.

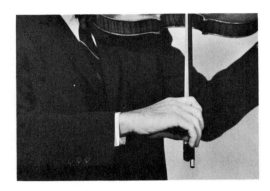

ILLUSTRATION 33   Setting the bow near the middle: "square position."

THE SQUARE (Illustration 33). The exact location of the square position varies somewhat from one individual to another, but it can be located easily by bending the elbow to form a right angle and then setting the bow on the strings so that it is parallel to the bridge. Approximately the middle of the bow will contact the strings in most cases, but with those whose arms are long from shoulder to elbow, the point of contact will move upward somewhat toward the tip. Forming the square with the bow resting on the G string and using the basic bow grip as described, the hand and forearm will then be lined up in approximately a level plane, roughly parallel to the floor. As each consecutive string is played, the plane of the stroke changes its angle with the floor, tilting more and more downward toward the right.

With the bow resting on the G string and the arm at the square position, the hand will then be in its neutral relationship with the arm; that is to say, it will be neither raised above the level of the wrist nor dropped below nor bent sideways. The square position, therefore, forms a starting position for free play in all directions.

In this position, the stick of the bow is very slightly tilted toward the fingerboard. The bow-hair crosses the string at a perfect right angle to the string's length. The player's shoulder must be completely relaxed at all costs, and should remain in this relaxed state throughout the drawing of the stroke from one end of the bow to the other. It is not only advisable, but also imperative, to stress shoulder relaxation *from the very beginning.*

THE SQUARE TO POINT (Illustration 34). To draw the bow successfully from the square to the point, as the bow-hand moves outward to the right, it must also push very gradually forward in approaching the tip of the stick in order to preserve the bow's

ILLUSTRATION 34   Setting the bow at the point.

parallel relationship with the bridge. This motion is performed by stretching the forearm and pushing forward with the upper arm.

The reason underlying the necessary forward motion rests in the circular character of the natural movements of the arm. As the point of the bow is approached, unless the upper arm *purposely* pushes forward, the lower arm will *naturally* describe a backward-moving arc as it opens up on the down-bow. This opening out of the arm at the elbow is not sufficient in itself to preserve the straightness of the stroke. The bow hand has to reach gradually frontward as the arm straightens. For the sake of brevity we have called this forward motion on the down-bow the "out" motion. Thus, from the square to the point, the bow moves *out* on the down-bow.

As the out motion takes place, the hand leans slightly to the left (pronation), thus adding a little more pressure to the bow and giving a small outward contour to the under side of the wrist. Any further precision adjustment that may be needed can then be made with the extended finger motion shown in Illustration 29 (pivotal motion, little finger pushing forward).

In returning up-bow from the point to the square, the motions are reversed. The elbow gradually bends, bringing the forearm from its straight-line position back to its right angle relationship, as the middle of the bow is approached. The upper arm begins to pull backward as the up-bow stroke starts. This backward motion we shall term the "in" motion. The hand and arm return to the square position.

Especially in playing in the upper half of the bow should one have a sensation of ease and freedom of motion in the forearm and elbow.

Players who have difficulty in negotiating the required outward (forward) reach as they approach the point of the bow will do well to try swinging the scroll of the instrument into a position pointing more nearly straight ahead instead of so far to the left. Conversely, players with long arms will often feel more comfortable when they hold the instrument farther to the left. With children, the difficulties of the outward reach are often aggravated by a bow that is too long. In this case, they should be given shorter bows or told not to use that section, near the point, which causes the trouble. This will not interfere in any way with their using the entire length later on when the arm has become sufficiently long.

THE SQUARE TO THE FROG. As the bow progresses from the square position to the frog, the elbow swings forward and the hand drops easily and naturally from the wrist. At the frog itself, the wrist becomes the slightly curved fulcrum or point of suspension, with the elbow freely hanging on one side and the bow-hand and bow on the other. In this position the bow and elbow counterbalance each other.

Moving up-bow from the square to the frog, the stick of the bow should tip gradually and slightly toward the fingerboard. This tilting accomplishes three things: (1) it preserves the straightness of the bow stroke as the frog is approached, since the arm is foreshortened as the hand gradually drops from the wrist; (2) it removes the inner edge of the hair from the strings, thus compensating for the natural increase of bow weight and pressure on the strings at the frog of the bow; (3) it contributes the correct type of bend and flexibility to the wrist-action.

One should take care not to exaggerate the tilting motion, since it can cause too high a wrist at the frog, which is very undesirable.

To achieve all of these necessary motions, the shoulder muscles must remain relaxed, the shoulder unshrugged, so that the upper arm is completely free to swing comfortably forward (toward the left) as the frog is approached. This forward motion can be seen clearly in the movement of the elbow, which describes a forward arc as the bow approaches the frog.

In bowing in either direction from the square (toward the point or toward the frog), the various elements of the motions have to be combined into a natural and harmonious unit. None should be over-emphasized, none left out. It is up to the player to see that a good balance is obtained with neither too much nor too little of each element.

For example, in approaching the frog an excessive raising of the wrist with a consequent excessive dropping of the hand will make the wrist form a right angle. This is definitely undesirable and will show a one-sided over-emphasis.

Equally injurious will be an excessive lateral bend of the wrist at the frog, a curving of the wrist toward the player's chin. This type of inward curve in the wrist is bound to tighten and cramp the functioning of the entire bowing unit. It is often encountered with players who have been taught to keep the wrist completely flat at the frog.

The slant of the instrument affects the appearance of the right elbow. Certain players hold the violin high in such a way that the top has very little inclination but is instead horizontal and parallel to the floor. Such players seem to have a high elbow without this actually being so. What is really important in this whole question is the interrelationship of the wrist, the elbow, and the position of the instrument, not merely the absolute height of the elbow itself. As long as the elbow (at the frog of the bow) is lower than the wrist, it cannot be considered a high elbow.

TONE PRODUCTION

Thus far we have established the fact that good tone production is dependent upon two things, the flexible springlike action of the arm and bow, and the motion of the stroke at right angles to the length of the string. These are fundamentals, but in no sense do they tell the whole story relative to tone production. It is now our purpose to discuss in more detail this important question.

The Three Main Factors: Speed, Pressure, and Sounding Point

Taking for granted a bow stroke moving parallel to the bridge, we must consider these three fundamental factors for the right hand: (1) the speed of the bow stroke, (2) the pressure it exerts on the strings, and (3) the point at which it contacts the string. This latter will be termed the *"sounding point."* These three factors are interdependent, inasmuch as a change in any one of them will require a corresponding adaptation in *at least one* of the others. How this interdependence works is briefly indicated in the following examples which, however, are not exhaustive in their coverage of the subject.

Increase of pressure with constant sounding point requires an increase of speed in the bow; decrease of pressure requires decrease of speed of stroke.

Increase of pressure with constant speed of bow stroke requires the sounding point to move toward the bridge.

Decrease of pressure with constant speed of bow requires the sounding point to move toward the fingerboard.

Greater speed with constant pressure requires the sounding point to move toward the fingerboard.

Slower speed with constant pressure requires a move toward the bridge.

In the foregoing examples one of the elements is always given as a constant. When change occurs in all three factors, a great variety of combinations can result. In the following paragraphs, each of these factors will be discussed individually.

SPEED. Greater speed of bow stroke per time unit means greater energy transmitted to the violin. If pressure (the other energy producing factor) remains constant, a change in speed will produce a change in dynamics: increase of speed will mean increase in sound; decrease of motion, decrease in sound. For a tone or a tone-sequence that requires the same dynamic throughout, the simplest and therefore the best way to bow is with equalized speed; this will also, under the circumstances, entail equal pressure and identical sounding point. Equal speed of the bow means, of course, equal division of the bow for equal time units. For instance, if four quarter notes are to be played within one whole bow, each single quarter note should be played with one-fourth of the bow. If there are a dotted half note and a quarter note, the dotted note will have to have three quarters of the bow and the second note one quarter. A well-controlled and logical division of the bow is of the greatest importance. When it is absent, unwanted dynamics or undesirable tone quality or both will be the result.

One of the most frequent faults found in this connection is that many players waste too much bow at the beginning of the stroke and therefore run out of bow toward the end. When this happens, such players start squeezing and pinching with the small remainder of the stroke resulting in a choking of the tone quality, coupled with an uneven dynamic rendition. Other players sometimes find too much bow left over at the end and, in an effort to use up the excess bow, give a sudden jerk with equally unfortunate results. Such bad effects are by no means limited to the two ends of the bow, for at any place in the bow's length a deficiently planned and executed division of the bow can cause undesirable accents, crescendos, decrescendos, and sudden unwanted changes of tone quality.

A special problem in connection with speed occurs in patterns like that in Example 37.

Example 37

If we want to stay in the same part of the bow, the speed of the up-bow will have to be three times as fast as that of the down-bow. Such changes in speed, imposed by certain rhythmic patterns, create some of the most difficult of bowing problems. (This will be discussed further on pages 86–7.) The immediate problem is that the sudden increase in speed produces an increase in sound. If such a dynamic change is not desired, then a quick adjustment has to be made by reducing the pressure for exactly the right amount to compensate for the increase in speed. This necessarily involves, also, a simultaneous move of the sounding point toward the fingerboard (pages 59–60).

Where the dynamic is not meant to be even—be it for outright accents, crescendos, the subtle nuance that is necessary for good phrasing, the little inflection that gives life to a single note, or whatever—a variation of speed in the stroke will be called for, mostly in combination with a corresponding increase in pressure. For example, on a four-beat steady-crescendo note, about one-third to one half of the bow should be saved for the last beat. Similarly, in phrasing, the climax note should have more bow, while the closing note, in tapering off as it ought to, will have less. Very delicate shadings can be obtained. These subtle manipulations of the bow speed realize them in the smoothest way possible.

PRESSURE. The pressure that the bow applies to the strings can derive either from the weight of the bow, the weight of the arm and hand, from controlled muscular action, or from a combination of these factors. The bow, being a lever, follows the ordinary principles of leverage. Its weight will be felt least at the tip and will increase gradually with the distance from the tip until it becomes heaviest at the frog. The same principle applies to the pressure that originates from muscular action or from the transfer of arm and hand weight; its effect will naturally decrease toward the point of the bow and increase toward the frog. An unhappy consequence of this lever characteristic is the violinistically-very-awkward fact that an equal pressure or weight *applied throughout the bow* results in an unequal pressure on the strings. Consequently, wherever an even dynamic is needed, the pressure-weight combination applied has to be uneven. The pressure must be stronger toward the point to counteract the loss of weight in the bow and correspondingly decreased toward the frog where the bow's weight is heaviest.

What counts in tone production is not just the amount of pressure used but, if one may so term it, the *quality* of the pressure. This is determined by the manner in which the pressure is transmitted. The main point is that it must not, under any circumstances, take effect as a dead weight, inelastic and inarticulate, that would crush the vibrations of the string or, at best, produce a tone of inferior quality. Instead the weight of the arm and hand and the pressure from the muscles should be transmitted through the flexible and well-coordinated system of springs, natural and artificial, which was outlined at the beginning of this chapter. These springs can transform weight or pressure into an impulse that makes the string respond in a manner that is thoroughly alive and susceptible to the finest modulations. All of the springs have to be working. Any stiffness in any joint between finger tips and shoulder is a spring "out of commission" that will hinder the transmission of energy. A rigid or shrugged shoulder, for instance, will eliminate the weight of the arm as a usable pressure element.

Any other rigidity will have no less deplorable an effect. The fewer springs there are in action and interaction, the more inflexible and unyielding becomes the whole system of pressure transmission.

Regarding the matter of firmness, the springs can be set, upon occasion, very firmly, but they must never become completely inflexible. The performer's choice of the right interplay of springs, the right setting of their firmness or looseness, the right proportion of muscular pressure and of arm and hand weight, cannot possibly be achieved by calculation. He cannot decide beforehand to apply so much pressure from this muscle, so much from that, so much weight from the bow, so much from the hand and arm, or to use this much springiness in finger knuckles or wrist, and so on. What is important is that the springs be in good working order and adaptable to various grades of flexibility, and that the whole right arm mechanism function as an organic unity. Thereafter, the musical imagination, desiring certain sounds, and the ear, listening attentively for positive results, will automatically bring forth the necessary coordination of all elements involved. Thus, listening ability becomes of paramount importance in finding the right procedure to adopt.

Before leaving this subject of pressure, it is pertinent to call attention to the fact that inaccurately controlled pressure can cause a change of pitch. In this way, faulty bow action affects the intonation.

SOUNDING POINT. The third main factor in tone production is the *sounding point*. We may define this term as that particular place, in relationship to the bridge, where the bow has to contact the string in order to get the best tonal results. That this point changes location with the varying speeds and pressures of the bow has already been established. It should now be added that some other factors in addition to speed and pressure have an influence on the location of the sounding point. These are the length, the thickness, and the tension of the string itself. It is not necessary to go into the physical basis for this. All that needs to be understood is the fact that on thinner strings the sounding point is closer to the bridge than on thicker strings and that in the higher positions the sounding point is also closer to the bridge than in the lower positions. This means, of course, that with every change from one string to another and with each shift of the left-hand position, the sounding point has to change, however slightly, if the speed and pressure of the bow are to remain the same. This fact brings with it a complication in the playing of double stops, especially if one of the two strings is being stopped at a place much closer to the bridge than the

other string. In such a case we have two distinct sounding
points, and obviously some kind of compromise will have to be
found. How to effect the compromise will depend on the musical context, whether one note is more important than the other.
In Example 38, for instance, it is obvious that the sounding point
for the D string has to be given more consideration than the one
for the G string.

Example 38
Mozart: *Concerto No. 4 in D major*
Rondo (measures 142–45)

With all of these many factors influencing the sounding point,
it would seem almost impossible to find the right sounding point
at any given moment. Yet like many another facet of the violinist's technique, which often seems very complicated, the solution here, too, is quite simple for those who have a good technical equipment, a good ear, and a sound musical instinct. Such
players will arrive at a degree of proficiency at which they apparently find the right sounding point instinctively by feeling
the way toward and away from the bridge. The prerequisite
for this is the technical ability first to find the sounding point
and then to know how to keep it and how to change it upon
demand. A player whose ear is not keen or not alert enough to
guide him to the best sounding point, or whose bow technique
does not allow him to follow his ear, will, of course, never
achieve satisfactory tone production. Generally, he will not
make even a barely passable tone unless he is constantly and
thoroughly trained over a period of time.

How to acquire skill in locating, in keeping, and in changing
the sounding point is outlined in the following exercises.

The basic technique required is the ability to *change* the point
of contact of the bow with the string. If this ability is lacking,
the correct sounding point can neither be sought out nor followed in its frequent moves between the bridge and fingerboard.

One method of varying the point of contact is to *glide* the
bow away from the bridge or to pull it toward the bridge in
such a way that it never relinquishes its right angle relationship
to the string (page 61). A second method makes use of the
fact that a stroke that is moving slightly nonparallel to the bridge
will permit the bow to slide toward or away from the fingerboard, depending upon the oblique direction it assumes.

On the down-bow, a turning of the point of the bow away from the bridge will cause the bow to slide toward the fingerboard, whereas turning in the opposite direction will cause the bow to slide toward the bridge. This applies to the down-bow stroke only. The reverse is true on the up-bow. Let us now suppose that the sounding point is to move toward the fingerboard on a down-bow, as it will, for example, in a diminuendo. In this case the point of the bow should be made to turn away from the bridge. This is accomplished by *not reaching far enough forward* with the bow hand as the tip is approached. As a result, the bow begins its slide toward the fingerboard. To move the bow toward the bridge, on the down-bow, the player will exaggerate the reaching forward of the bow hand as the stroke nears the point of the bow, thus making the tip turn in toward the bridge. In the up-bow these methods are reversed.

After achieving facility in this moving of the bow from one point of contact to another, it is best to proceed to exercises for the *exact location*, maintenance, and precise change of the sounding point.

First, it is good to start with a long note, bowing slowly with a rather heavy pressure and seeking a place near the bridge where the most resonant sound is produced. Having located this correct sounding point, continue to draw the bow with the same amount of pressure but with a gradually increasing *speed of stroke*, in the meantime following the sounding point on its move *toward the fingerboard*. Listen for the same resonant sound throughout.

Second, take a similar exercise, but this time start with a light pressure and use fairly fast strokes. Find the best sounding point (which under these conditions will be away from the bridge and nearer the fingerboard). Gradually increase the pressure *without changing the speed of the strokes*. With the speed constant, the sounding point will move *toward the bridge*.

Next, take an exercise using a dotted half note on the down-bow followed by a quarter note on the up-bow. Balance the sound so that they are of equal loudness. (See also the exercises for the *son filé* in the chapter On Practicing, page 103.) In the present exercise, more pressure has to be put on the half note and less on the quarter note. The sounding point for the shorter note is closer to the fingerboard.

Now, vary this exercise by using a five-count note followed by a one-count note, the first down-bow, the second up-bow. Then reverse and start up-bow on the long note, taking the short note down-bow. Balance the tone on each stroke.

Finally, practice a quarter note, half note, quarter note sequence, in which the bow will have to approach the bridge on the half note.

Work all of these exercises, first keeping the same amount of sound throughout: all forte, all piano. Then try varying the dynamic thus: one note piano, the next forte, and so on. Many other combinations of a similar nature will suggest themselves. Attention might be called to the fact that the *glide* of the bow (shifting the sounding point immediately while retaining the right angle contact with the string) is of especial value in the instant change from forte to piano and vice versa. The glide technique should be used here.

Having gone through these exercises, practice the *son filé*— the very long sustained tone. Keep the length of the notes the same, using a whole bow for each note and holding it as long as possible. Change the dynamic from one note to the next in this manner: pianissimo on the first note, piano on the next, then mezzo piano, mezzo forte, forte, fortissimo; then gradually return to the pianissimo by reverse steps. Continuous contact must be maintained with the most resonant sounding point.

Each of the foregoing exercises should be played first on one single pitch throughout the exercise. Afterwards, it is recommended that these exercises be practiced in different positions, with varying notes, including the crossing of strings, since all of these factors influence the location of the sounding point, as was explained before.

The Slightly Slanted Stroke

It was stated previously that the perfectly straight bow stroke is the foundation of all bowing technique. Until now it has been assumed that the bow is perfectly parallel to the bridge at all times. However, it is a fact that in drawing a singing tone at not too great a speed, the most resonant sound will be produced when the bow is at an *extremely* slight angle with the bridge— in such a fashion that the point of the bow is always a little more toward the fingerboard and the frog slightly closer to the player's body. The bow thus takes an ever-so-slight turn in the clockwise direction. The angle of slant is always the same and does not change from down-bow to up-bow. Technically, the bow should follow an identical path on both strokes, down and up.

A slant in the opposite direction, the point nearer the bridge and the frog farther away, produces generally inferior tonal results. The facts as stated here can be confirmed by anybody whose ear is sensitive to shades of resonance and color. It is the ear that has to be the judge of when and in what amount the slant should be applied.

Character and Color of the Tone; Various Styles of Tone Production

We have seen how a certain pressure and speed determine the location of the sounding point for any given note and how a certain chosen sounding point combined with a certain speed determine the necessary pressure, and so on. The understanding of this relationship is of great importance, but it must not lead to the false belief that there is only one combination of the three factors possible in any given instance. In most cases the player has several possibilities to choose from as far as the mixing of the basic factors is concerned. The several choices result in various styles of tone production. For simplicity's sake, we shall reduce these to two main types that are the most characteristic.

Type One relies mainly on speed to bring out the dynamic differences required in the music; consequently, much bow will be used without too much pressure. The sounding point will have a tendency to be farther away from the bridge.

Type Two relies mainly on pressure, which will be used in combination with a rather slow speed in the bow and a resulting tendency for the sounding point to hover in the neighborhood of the bridge.

These two types differ as to the character of the color in the sound. A tone produced with much bow and little pressure has a light, loose character; one produced with much pressure and little speed has a quality of denseness and concentration. In addition, the accompanying change in the position of the sounding point in itself brings about a change in color: the nearer the bridge, the brighter the color, the more incisive the timbre; in the neighborhood of the fingerboard, the color is paler, more delicate and pastel-like.

There is hardly a finished violinist who will at all times adhere strictly to only one of these types. But there are a great many whose style of tone production will always stay very close to a single type, never straying very far away from it. Those who do so limit severely the expressive scope of their playing. Every violinist is well advised to master not only these two basic types but to learn to mix them in all sorts of combinations and thereby to achieve command over a wide range of sound-character and timbre.

If, in addition to the foregoing variations in coloring, one uses at will the several types of vibrato with their different shadings, then it becomes clear that the possible combinations are innumerable and can yield an infinitely diversified palette of the most varied character, color, and quality of sound.

Faulty Tone Production

Whenever anything is done that is contrary to the principles of good tone production, whether it be to use a crooked bow stroke or a wrong combination of the three basic factors, the result will be an undesirable tone quality that can range from scratching and rasping to whistling and squeaking. Apart from such obvious faults, tone production can also be defective because of the wrong setting of the natural springs and a resulting wrong combination of pressure and weight factors.

Two main types of defect are frequently found: the tight sound and the very loose sound. The first results when the springs in the fingers are too firm, the latter when they are too loose.

To loosen the springs in the tight sound, it will help most to play a fast, light tremolo with very short strokes near the very point of the bow with only the index finger and the thumb holding the bow and the other fingers removed from contact with the bow. When the feeling of greater looseness is well established in the hand and fingers, one should then proceed to play with a détaché stroke in the upper half of the bow, in the same fashion, with only the index finger and the thumb holding the bow. When this can be done with ease, the other fingers should be replaced on the bow without pressure, the détaché continued, and the attention centered on a singing quality of tone. This same exercise is very helpful in improving the quality of the double piano. Refer to Illustration 24, page 47.

A frequent cause for the tight sound is a bow grip in which the index finger and the second finger hold the stick too close to their tips. This grip, in strong dynamics, requires an overdose of muscular pressure and, therefore, has a tightening effect on the springs. In such a case the bow should be held deeper in the hand, with the fingers contacting the stick farther from the nails and closer to the middle joints. This will permit a loosening of the springs and a better utilization of the weight factor with a corresponding reduction of pressure as such. Holding the wrist slightly higher and using less pressure on the strings will also help to overcome this particular tonal trouble.

If the sound is too loose, the opposite should be done: the springs, especially those of the fingers, should be tightened and some pressure added by the fingers and the hand, thus returning weight to the strings. One should try to keep the wrist toward the right with a feeling of *pulling* the bow, the wrist leading in both the down-bow and up-bow directions. The wrist should not be lowered.

BOWING PATTERNS

In the following survey of bowings I have tried to list and describe those characteristic patterns of execution that can be considered basic types. This is, by no means, a complete catalogue, since these basic types can be mixed to form a great variety of new patterns.

The principles already discussed, regarding the straight bow stroke (the "direction—out, in"), the system of springs, and the tone production with its relationship of speed, pressure, and sounding point, *apply to all of the various bowings*.

Legato (*Marking:* ⌐⌐⌐⌐)

In the slurring of two or more notes on one bow stroke, which is called the *legato*, we are faced with two main problems. One is concerned with the change of fingers in the left hand, the other with the change of strings. Considering the finger problem, we see that the basic need is that the bow must not be disturbed by what the left hand is doing. If difficulties are present on this account, it is advisable to practice an exercise of the type quoted in Example 39, in which the notes to be fingered are immaterial and can be varied at discretion.

Example 39

On these slurs, the feeling in the bow arm should be the same as for the open string whole notes.

A certain complication arises when the fingering during a slur involves a substantial change of position. This will not only require a change of sounding point, but will frequently also call for the bow's assistance in making the major shift. This skill was discussed in the section devoted to Shifting, pages 23–27. It involves a slight slowing down of the bow stroke and a gentle lifting of the pressure during the motion of the left hand. If this is done, it has to be carefully effected so that the gain in camouflaging the slide is not more than offset by a too audible disruption of the legato flow.

As soon as more than one string is involved in the slur, the second problem of the legato presents itself: i.e., the change of strings on the slurred bow stroke. As a rule, a smooth change of strings is best effected by a subtle, *close approach to the new string* in the fashion demonstrated in Example 40.

If the crossing is made gradually enough, a double stop will sound momentarily between the two notes, as indicated by the grace note in the example. This double stop should form so subtly that it is not possible to distinguish either the exact moment of its beginning or the instant of its termination. In the example, the E gradually fades out as the C begins to be heard. A very slight pressure of the bow, just as the crossing is made, will help further in binding the tones smoothly together.

Where the bow changes back and forth between two strings many times on one bow stroke, it should stay as close as possible to both strings without sacrificing the clear articulation of each note (Example 41).

Example 40

Example 41
Beethoven: *Concerto in D major*, Op. 61
Finale: Rondo (measures 224–25)

String crossings of this type are hardest when they are close to the frog, and special attention should therefore be devoted to their practice in the lower and lowest part of the bow. For the section nearest the frog, the finger action shown in Illustration 30 (down, up) in conjunction with the forearm rotation (page 50) is to be used. As the bow moves toward the point, the motion gradually goes over into the vertical (down, up) motion of the hand shown in Illustration 31. This swinging of the hand at the wrist replaces the other motions at the tip of the bow.

Complete smoothness in changing strings will not always be desirable in legato (slurred) playing. Where a rather percussive finger-articulation is indicated (as, for instance, in a loud scale or arpeggio run), a too-smooth change of string on the part of the bow will disturb the unity of the passage, because the smoothness of the change of string will be out of character with the articulation of the rest of the notes by the left hand. It is important, therefore, to see to it that the legato string crossings *match in sound the percussion of the left hand fingers*. Such articulated string crossings should be applied in cases like those shown in Examples 1, page 14, and 42, page 66.

Example 42

Lalo: *Symphonie espagnole*, Op. 21
First movement (measures 65–66)

* Articulate the changes of string with the bow.

† Articulate by lifting the preceding finger, half pizzicato, in a sideways direction.

The run, in general, is played with articulation in the fingers. Thus, all three types of articulation are shown in this example.

Example 43

Bruch: *Concerto in G minor*, Op. 26
First movement (measures 88–89)

Defects in legato string crossings can also be caused by faulty coordination of the bow with the left hand. The most common errors are those in which the finger on the note preceding the crossing is lifted too soon, or the finger on the note after the crossing is not prepared soon enough. In Example 43, the fourth finger must not be lifted until after the bow has left the G string. The first finger must be *already firmly in place* at the instant the bow touches the D string, the note E already depressed to the fingerboard.

Coordination problems created by fast passages with string crossings can best be approached by first isolating the string-change pattern and then practicing it on the open strings. The second measure in Example 43, for instance, will yield to the string-change pattern shown under Example 44.

Example 44

Example 43 (second measure)
as a bowing study

If the difficulty is not so much with the coordination of the two hands as it is with the sound of the passage, it will help to play, first, an open string (or the *first* note of the passage) several times with a full, round, long, and fluent tone and then, in proceeding to the run itself, to try to maintain the same feeling of fluency in the right arm. Such a technique is demonstrated on Example 43 as shown in Example 45.

Example 45
Example 43 (second measure)
as a tone study

Détaché

THE SIMPLE DÉTACHÉ (No special marking). A separate bow is taken for each note and the stroke is smooth and even throughout with *no variation* of pressure. There is no break between the notes, and each bow stroke has, therefore, to be continued until the next takes over. The simple détaché can be played in any part of the bow and with any length of stroke from the whole bow to the smallest fraction (Example 46).

Example 46
Bach: *Partita No. 1 in B minor*
Last double: beginning

The execution of the simple détaché will vary according to the length of the stroke, the speed, and the dynamic. With a stroke that is fairly long and not too fast, the movement as described for the drawing of the straight bow will apply. The faster the stroke, the less the arm will participate in the action.

When there is a constant reiteration of string crossing, as in Example 47, the motion is made either by the vertical movement of the hand (Illustration 31) or by the forearm rotation (pronation-supination) or by both combined, depending upon the section of the bow used.

Exercises for the reiterated string crossings, which are numerous among the violin etudes, should be practiced extensively, since they afford the best means of acquiring flexibility in the wrist.

Example 47
Bach: *Partita No. 3 in E major*
First movement: Prelude (measure 5)

THE ACCENTED OR ARTICULATED DÉTACHÉ (Marking: $\bar{F}$). In this bowing pattern each stroke starts with an accent or articulation that is produced, in its application here, by a sudden increase in both pressure and speed, without resorting to the martelé-type of "pinching" of the string (page 71). The stroke will almost always be continuous with no air-space between the

Example 48
Bach: *Partita No. 2 in D minor*
Chaconne (measure 169)

Example 49
Prokofiev: *Concerto No. 2 in G minor*, Op. 63
First movement (measures 138–39)

Example 50
Mendelssohn: *Concerto in E minor*, Op. 64
First movement (measures 139–42)

Example 51

notes, but exceptions do occur. An excerpt for the application of this stroke is quoted in Example 48.

THE DÉTACHÉ PORTÉ (Marking: ⌐). This stroke has a slight swelling at the beginning followed by a gradual lightening of the sound, similar to the portato or louré (below). This swelling is brought about by going somewhat deeper into the string by applying a carefully graded additional pressure and speed at the beginning of each note, without actually accenting it. There may or may not be a slight spacing between notes, but even when this stroke is performed continuously the inflections will give the impression of separations. This type of détaché is used to give more expression either to a group of détaché notes or to certain specific notes within such passages, thus putting them into better relief. Example 49 shows the independent use of this stroke.

THE PORTATO OR LOURÉ (Marking: ⌐ ⌐ ⌐). The portato or louré, while not, strictly speaking, one of the détaché bowings, is, nevertheless, so closely related in its execution to the détaché porté that it is not unwise to discuss it at this time. The louré is, in fact, nothing but a series of détaché porté strokes performed on one and the same bow stroke. On each note, exactly as in the porté itself, there is the initial swell followed by a gradual decrease in sound. The inflections may follow one another without a stop, and, in this form, the stroke is used to bring slurred legato notes into more expressive relief, or the single notes may be slightly separated, in which case their *sound*, in louré, is the same as that of the détaché porté where no slur exists. If the louré is executed with stops between the notes, the bow may either stay on the string or be lifted very gently from the string between notes. Example 50 shows the use of this bowing.

It is a very useful exercise to practice the portato (louré) mixed with the détaché porté, as shown in Example 51, and to balance their respective sounds.

THE DÉTACHÉ LANCÉ (Marking: ⌐). This is a rather short, quick stroke that is characterized by great *initial* speed in the bow which then slows down toward the end of the stroke. Generally, there is a clear break between the notes, although sometimes, as in a succession of fast notes, no pause will intervene. There is neither accent nor swell at the beginning of the tone. The stroke could be likened to a martelé without the staccato attack at the beginning. The détaché lancé can be used independently for passages that call for short strokes without any inflection as in Examples 52 and 53. However, it is used most often and most effectively in combination with the porté when the latter highlights the execution of a particular note or of several notes.

Example 52: The Détaché Lance
Bach: *Partita No. 1 in B minor*
Second double: beginning

When mixing is used, the notes between the two types specified will take the form of a transition and thereby partake of the character of both to some extent. Such mixing is, of course, not limited to lancé and porté but applies to all détaché patterns and in a wider sense, as we shall see, to all types of bowings. It may be stated that especially in extended passages of détaché one rarely encounters a single particular type of détaché that remains "pure" for any length of time. The more inventiveness a violinist displays in the selection and combination of the types and in the transition from one type to another (in the service of better phrasing and more expressive nuance), the more colorful and alive his playing style will be.

**Example 53: Détaché lancé
in combination with détaché porté**
Bach: *Sonata No. 1 in G minor*
Second movement: Fugue (measure 47)

All détaché bowings that have a break between the notes (especially the lancé and porté) can help to mold a musical phrase even more by the simple device of varying the length of the rests between the strokes. Although playing strictly in time by starting each note exactly on its beat, the variation of length in the spacing between notes can give an effective illusion of rubato playing. This is illustrated in Example 54.

Example 54

The Fouetté or Whipped Bow (Marking: ⸕)

The whipped or fouetté bowing is derived from the accented détaché, but here the accent is produced by quickly (and barely) lifting the bow off the string and striking it down again with suddenness and energy. It is generally performed in the upper half of the bow, mostly starting up-bow, and should be practiced first in that manner. It must also be mastered, however, on the down-bow.

Students trying to perfect this stroke generally make the mistake of lifting the bow too soon. The lift has to take place not at the end of the stroke just completed but so shortly before the beginning of the new stroke that the lifting and slapping down occur almost simultaneously. The whipped stroke has a quality of biting incisiveness. Its uses are many. It can be very effective when a note needs an accent and there is not time enough to pinch the string for a martelé attack (Example 55).

Example 55
Beethoven: *Concerto in D major,* Op. 61
Finale: Rondo (measures 68–69)

The whipped stroke also finds an excellent use when certain notes in a continuous détaché passage need to be both short and accented as, for instance, in Example 56.

Example 56
Wieniawski: *Concerto in D Minor,* Op. 22
Last movement: à la zingara
(measures 272–74)

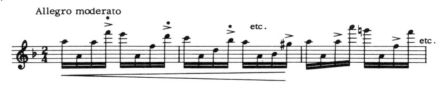

Example 57
Tartini: *Devil's Trill Sonata*
Second movement (measures 21–23
after double bar)

Another characteristic use of this bowing is in the accenting of short trills as in Example 57.

Martelé (Marking: ┌)

This is one of the most fundamental of all strokes, and its mastery will benefit the right hand technique well beyond the limit of this particular bowing. The détaché in particular will be helped by a good martelé, as will other bowings yet to be discussed, such as the collé, the staccato, and so on.

The martelé is decidedly a percussive stroke with a consonant type of sharp accent at the beginning of each note and always a rest between strokes. The accent in this stroke requires preparation in the form of preliminary pressure: the bow has to "pinch" the string before starting to move. This pinching is a pressure stronger than the stroke itself will require, and it has to last just long enough to produce the necessary accentuation at the beginning of the tone. The pressure is then immediately lessened to the degree required. If this preparatory pressure is released too soon, there will not be any accent; if it is released too late, there will be a scratch. The correct execution is therefore mainly a problem of timing and coordination.

Two fundamental types of martelé can be distinguished according to whether the actual note following the accent is to be short or long. The first can be called the *simple* martelé; the second, the *sustained* martelé.

THE SIMPLE MARTELÉ (Marking: ⌐). The simple or fast martelé can be played with any amount of bow from the whole length to the smallest part, and it may be played in any section of the bow from frog to point. When most of the pressure is not released at the termination of the stroke, the quality of the martelé suffers. However, not all of the pressure can be released, especially on the down-bow strokes, or the bow may jump off the string. The scratchy sound produced by too much pressure at the instant of stopping or by the application of pressure too early before the next stroke should always be avoided. Special care has to be taken not to apply new pressure before the stroke is finished, or the bow will come to a grinding stop. If an up-bow ends very near the frog, it is best to lift the bow slightly and then reset it for the next stroke, because it is very hard to avoid such a terminal scratch at the frog where there is great bow weight.

Since the preparation of the martelé requires considerable pressure, especially near the point of the bow, the hand and arm should be set in a way that is most suitable for the transmission of pressure and weight: the wrist should be somewhat lower and the forearm slightly pronated. In this setting, the base knuckles of the fingers are lowered a little.

At the frog, the bow has to be fully supported, and one must beware of over-pressing. The real action will, in all but the smallest strokes, originate in the whole arm, but it is hardly necessary to add that the fingers and hand must be flexible and yielding, true to their nature as springs. The shorter the stroke and the lighter the dynamic, the more the hand and fingers will become active. The small martelé strokes can be performed with the fingers and the hand alone. Contrarily, in big strokes it is important to keep in mind that the fingers set the pressure but *never start* the motion itself, which is actually begun by the arm. The fingers, whose contribution is at best very small, have to act concurrently with the arm but never ahead of it. There are then, three principal elements involved in the action: (1) the motion of the arm, (2) the horizontal finger motion (Illustration 28), and (3) the pressure of the fingers on the stick of the bow for the bite in the sound. (*Note:* the fingers are curved to start the down-bow martelé and straighten simultaneously with the bow's motion. On the up-bow, they begin with the straighter position and resume instantly the small curve.)

The amount of pressure to be applied before and the amount used during the stroke have to be discovered by experiment until, in the course of the learning, a natural and subconscious feeling for this technique is developed. Too much tension during the actual stroke, largely a carry-over from the necessary tension during the pinching of the string, will produce an ugly sound and will make the bow either bounce or kick back at the end of the stroke. One must watch carefully to see that the initial pressure-release brings with it a corresponding release in the muscular tension in the arm itself. An exception may be made for fast sequences of notes where the available time does not permit any relaxation of pressure to occur between notes. In these cases the quality of the sound produced has to be given special attention. Apart from too much pressure, too little pressure or an uneven application of it can also be a disturbing element.

When a large section of the bow is used, such as a half or a whole bow, the problem of direction becomes acute. The movement in the martelé is so fast that the student often fails to make all the adjustments that are required to keep the bow moving in an entirely straight path, parallel to the bridge. Yet absolute straightness is imperative and must be achieved. Care must be taken, too, that the sounding point is exactly right. Some of the difficulties encountered stem from the fact that many players are too concerned with the pressure factors and the rhythmic quality of the stroke and therefore neglect to concentrate on the quality of the sound produced.

The necessity for the pressure-preparation before each martelé stroke sets a definite speed limit on its proper use. When playing short strokes at the point, this limit can be somewhat extended by turning the bow so that the stick tilts slightly toward the bridge instead of toward the fingerboard. When the speed of any passage goes beyond the practical limit of the martelé, the latter has to be replaced either by the firm staccato, the collé, the whipped bow, or the accented détaché.

The martelé should be practiced with long rests between notes. It is best to start with a rather short stroke not exceeding a quarter of the bow in length.

When the martelé is combined with the crossing of strings, as in Example 58, the bow should, upon completion of any one stroke, *come to rest immediately on the string that is to be played next.*

The use of the quick martelé is shown in Examples 59, 60 and 61. The whole bow is to be used in Example 59, the approxi-

Example 58
Rudolphe Kreutzer: *42 studies*
No. 7: beginning

Example 59
Saint-Saëns: *Concerto in B minor,* Op. 61
First movement (measures 29–30)

Example 60
Brahms: *Concerto in D major,* Op. 77
First movement (measures 3–4 of the solo)

Example 61
Jacques-Pierre Joseph Rode: *24 Caprices*
No. 11 (measure 5)

mate half bow in Example 60, and the very short bow in Example 61.

THE SUSTAINED MARTELÉ (Marking:). The sustained martelé is an expressive détaché stroke that has a martelé start. Everything that has been said about the martelé attack applies here too. As soon as the attack is articulated, the short, rhythmic note of the fast martelé is replaced by a long sustained tone. Although the bow has to leave the martelé attack with a certain speed to avoid scratching, almost immediately thereafter the bow can slow down to any desired rate of speed. The use of this bowing is shown in Example 62.

Example 62
Brahms: *Concerto in D major,* Op. 77
Last movement (measures 57–63)

The Collé (No marking)

In the collé, the bow is placed on the strings from the air and at the moment of contact the string is lightly but sharply pinched. Simultaneously with the pinch, the note is attacked, and after the instantaneous sounding of the note the bow is immediately slightly lifted off the string in preparation for the next stroke. The pinch is very similar to the martelé attack except for the fact that the time of preparation is reduced to a minimum. It is in action, though not in sound, not unlike the plucking of the string, making, as it were, a pizzicato with the bow.

The collé is used in the lower half of the bow, and the length can vary from extremely small to fairly broad. It should be practiced first with as little bow as possible near the frog, then in the other parts of the bow, including, for study purposes, even the upper half. In such a very short stroke as the collé, only the fingers are active, the vertical motion of Illustration 27 for setting and pinching and the horizontal motion of Illustration 28 for sounding the note. This bowing should first be done with great lightness, the bow being placed on the strings with the ease of a bird alighting. Later the stroke can be lengthened with the arm leading and the fingers maintaining their just-described motion. Finally, it may be practiced with stronger dynamics.

A good method for initial practice is to start with a very light and a very short martelé stroke about three to four inches from the frog, lifting the bow immediately after each stroke and placing it back toward the frog a little to prepare for the next martelé attack. The time for preparation is gradually shortened until there is scarcely any preparation on the string, and the setting, pinching, and sounding practically coincide.

The collé is a very important practice bowing, invaluable for acquiring control of the bow in all of its parts. Added to this, it is musically very useful as a stroke that combines the lightness and grace of the spiccato with the incisiveness of the martelé. Played at the frog, it gives the same sound-effect as a light martelé played at the point and, in general, can replace the martelé when the tempo is too fast for the latter. The collé can give more emphasis to certain notes in a spiccato passage and can be used as an aid to slowing down the spiccato bowing when necessary.

In the broad collé, the arm comes into play. This bowing can replace the heavy spiccato advantageously. Examples 63 and 64 give passages where the collé may be used effectively.

Example 63
Brahms: *Concerto in D. major,* Op. 77
Last movement (measures 20–21)

Example 64
Beethoven: *Sonata in C minor*, Op. 32,
No. 2.
First movement (measures 35–37)

Spiccato (*Marking:* ♪♪♪♪)

In this type of execution, the bow is dropped from the air and leaves the string again after every note. In doing so it describes an arc-like motion that can be represented thus: ⌣ . The bow contacts the string at or near the bottom of the arc. The movement has both a horizontal and a vertical component. If the horizontal component is emphasized more than the vertical one, then the arc will be flatter: ⌣. In this case, the tone will have more substance and will be rounder, softer, more vowel-like. If the vertical component is more prominent, the arc is narrower and deeper: ⌣ , and consequently the tone is sharper, more accented, and percussive. Tone quality and dynamics will also be influenced by the height of the drop: the higher the starting point, the louder and, in general, the sharper will be the resulting sound.

In length, the spiccato can run the gamut from very short to very broad. It is used mainly in the lower two-thirds of the bow: when broad and slow, more towards the lower part; when fast and short, more towards the middle or even slightly above the middle. A characteristic type of short and sharp spiccato can, however, be played entirely at the frog by dropping the bow almost vertically. A spiccato at or near the point is possible, but it can be only the vertical type, and such a usage is pertinent solely where this special sound effect is desired. Its most appropriate use is in the midst of a left-hand pizzicato passage for the notes that cannot be plucked.

A general characteristic of the spiccato is that the bow is thrown down on the strings for every single note and (at least for the longer strokes) lifted up again. In a short and fairly fast spiccato the bow will come off the string by rebound, which may or may not have to be supplemented by further lifting. As far as the dropping on the string is concerned, there always has to be an individual impulse for every tone, and because of this there is a definite speed limit beyond which the spiccato becomes impractical.

Because the starting position of the bow, in this stroke, is in the air, the bow has to be supported throughout, which means that the arm and wrist ought to be held slightly higher. (This is accomplished by swinging the elbow outward a little from the side of the body. Guard against shrugging the shoulder.)

The main impulse for the action comes from the arm, but hand and fingers participate in a partly active, partly passive way with a combination of the vertical and the horizontal motions for the hand (Illustration 31) and the vertical motion of the fingers (Illustration 27). In case of need, some horizontal pivoting adjustment in the fingers (Illustration 29) has to be added for the sake of straightening the stroke in the right direction. The greater the speed, the more the center of action will shift from the arm toward the hand and fingers.

It is very important to listen to the tone quality and to try to obtain a resonant sound. Therefore, it is advisable in most cases to stress the horizontal element rather than the vertical; in other words, to use generally more bow and not let it jump too high. The direction of the bow has to be watched, and the weight, speed, and sounding point must be adjusted in just the right way for the resonant fullness of sound that is desirable. In the concert hall especially, violinists will be well advised to avoid the use of the too-steep and too-percussive spiccato. Although it might sound fairly good at close range, it does not carry properly because of lack of vowel quality.

When crossing the strings in spiccato, care must be taken to keep the same amount of bow hair in contact with the string, or the spiccato will become uneven. The bow should remain close to the strings during the crossing, since the likelihood of losing control becomes greater the higher the bounce goes before crossing. This action across strings should be performed primarily with the whole arm plus the addition of the forearm rotation, hand and fingers participating slightly.

When the spiccato gets very broad and the tone becomes long enough to acquire a bit of singing quality, one can call it the "singing spiccato." This sound bears the same relationship to the regular spiccato that the détaché porté has to the simple variety of détaché, or the sustained martelé to the short type. The singing spiccato can, of course, be applied to a whole phrase, but it will be especially effective when it is used for the expressive emphasis of a certain note within a regular spiccato passage.

When the spiccato is mixed with détaché bowings, the latter will be used to underline what needs to be emphasized.

A more percussive spiccato is known as the accented variety. The height of the drop is raised, and the width of the stroke is shortened.

It is best to start the practice of the spiccato in the lower part of the bow with broad, flat strokes describing a shallow arc, the arm leading and the hand and fingers following and kept very flexible. When this is good, one can then use shorter strokes more toward the middle of the bow, adding thereto somewhat more of the vertical element.

After learning to execute the various individual types of spiccato at different speeds and dynamic shades, one should proceed to practice the gradual transition from singing to regular to accented and back. Finally, all types should be practiced by mixing them in different combinations *without transition* but by direct change from one to another.

Sautillé (Marking: ＼)

This is another jumping bowing, which is distinguished from the spiccato by the fact that there is no *individual* lifting and dropping of the bow for each note. The task of jumping is left principally to the resiliency of the stick. This bowing is best when played around the middle of the bow, somewhat lower when it is slower and louder, somewhat higher when it is faster and softer. The choice of place will differ with different bows owing to their dissimilar conditions of elasticity. Contrary to common belief, the sautillé stroke may be played from very fast to quite slow, although in slow tempos the spiccato will generally be the more practical choice.

To practice the sautillé, start with a small and fairly fast détaché near the middle of the bow, then turn the stick perpendicularly above the hair so that all of the hair contacts the string. Hold the bow lightly and center the action in the fingers which perform a combination of the vertical and horizontal finger motions (Illustrations 27 and 28) in an *oblique* direction about half way between these two movements. To this is added a similar combination of vertical and horizontal actions in the hand (page 50) which follows passively. For the sautillé, the forearm is slightly more pronated than for the spiccato, and the balance point of the hand rests entirely on the index finger, with the second and third fingers only slightly touching the bow. The fourth finger, which is very active in spiccato in balancing the bow, has no function at all in the sautillé and has to remain completely passive without any pressure on the stick.

The sautillé may fail to jump properly off the string if it is attempted at a wrong place in the bow, but actually when trouble occurs it is more often caused by a heavy grip of the third and fourth fingers. To make sure that this does not happen, it is best first to practice by holding the bow only between

Example 65

the first finger and thumb. Only after the stroke is functioning in this fashion should the second and third fingers be put back in place again on the stick. The fourth finger may or may not be returned to the stick.

If there is difficulty in making the sautillé jump sufficiently, the exercise given in Example 65 will help.

This type of practice will stress a little more the vertical components of the finger and hand motions. If, on the other hand, the bow jumps too much, then a little more pressure should be given with the index finger. It might also help to revert temporarily to the small, short détaché from which the sautillé was derived. The short détaché can often very successfully replace the sautillé, especially when the tempo is rather fast. Although the bow does not leave the strings under these circumstances, it can be made to resemble closely the sound of a fast sautillé.

Staccato (Marking:  *)*

This bowing, most often used as the "solid staccato" in contrast to the "flying staccato," is a succession of short, clearly separated, and consonant-articulated strokes on one bow, performed while the hair of the bow remains in permanent contact with the string. It is practiced most of the time as a series of small, successive martelé strokes that follow one another in the same direction of the bow, either up or down. The bow is set firmly for each stroke, and the pressure is released after the accent has sounded on each note. Practiced in this manner, however, the staccato cannot exceed by very much the speed limit that is characteristic of the martelé itself; but in musical usage the staccato as such can (and usually has to) be played faster than the martelé. In this faster tempo, we find today (in actual practice) very many different ways in which this bowing is being performed. If a student has a staccato that sounds good and is under fairly good rhythmic control, the teacher should, by all means, leave it alone, even if it is performed in an unusual way. The solid staccato is a very personal type of bowing.

When played fast, the staccato is based on tenseness coupled with the muscular oscillations in the arm, hand and/or fingers brought about by this tenseness. The rate of oscillation varies with the individual. It is too fast in some and too slow in others to be of practical value. But where the oscillations are within the useful range, the student should be encouraged to experiment with all kinds of finger, hand, and arm adjustments to find the way in which the muscular tremblings can best be transformed into good staccato bowing. If he has difficulty in doing this, it will help greatly on the up-bow to bring the arm "in" more, i.e., pull the arm closer to the body so that the bow will not cut the string at a perfect right angle but will instead take a slight turn in the clockwise direction. Also, he should try to raise the elbow, pronate the forearm, and tilt the stick more toward the fingerboard. The opposite is done for the down-bow staccato: the arm is moved "out" more during the strokes so that the bow takes a little turn in the counterclockwise direction; the wrist is lowered much and the elbow a little; and the bow stick is tilted toward the bridge. The forearm is completely pronated for the down-bow staccato. For ultimate speed, the arm muscles have to be tightened; the hair placed firmly on the string and kept there solidly with no release of pressure between notes.

The speed of the tense staccato will, in the beginning, be the one that the player's natural tension produces spontaneously, and the practice effort has to be focused on getting it under control and on varying the rate of reiteration, slowing it down if it is too fast, and speeding it up if it is too slow. A staccato that can be performed only at a very slow or an exaggeratedly fast tempo is of very little musical value.

There are two principal difficulties in staccato. One is the motion itself. The other is the coordination with the left hand fingers and the string changes. These two problems should be approached separately. The staccato should first be practiced on one single note in order to get the movement under control in its action, rhythm, and speed. It is best to work it in small sections of two, three, four, five, and more notes, as well as in some rhythmical patterns (Example 66).

Example 66

When the movement begins to work, the left hand finger-changes are introduced, and finally changes of strings in all kinds of scale and arpeggio patterns are added. Here it will be discovered that the up-bow staccato is somewhat easier on descending than on ascending scales, the down-bow staccato considerably easier in the ascending motion and quite difficult in the descending direction.

The tense staccato has to be practiced with caution. The time spent in uninterrupted practice should be limited, or the unrelieved tension may have harmful results. Consequently, extended periods of regular daily practice are not to be recommended: it is far better to interrupt the general practice routine for a few minutes of tense staccato practice now and then, returning afterward to other practice materials.

In the moderate speeds, the tension method will still work best for many players, although the center for the muscular tension may shift from the upper arm more toward the forearm. However, many violinists will be able to dispense either partly or entirely with the tension and substitute a looser and even a rather relaxed motion of the hand, mostly in the lateral direction with the fingers and thumb following flexibly. Others may use a rotation of the forearm that is possible only when the bow is well suspended from the hand, and the forearm is turned somewhat toward the right in supination. Still others can obtain a fine staccato motion by a vertical shaking movement of the fingers. If the hand motion itself is used, it will often help in initial practice to lift the second and fourth fingers off the stick, thus freeing the hand for the lateral motion (Illustration 35).

In the down-bow staccato it is sometimes useful to practice the stroke holding the bow with only the index finger and the thumb, the stick tipped toward the player.

The field of experimentation is very wide for those who have trouble starting the staccato motion, but, in general, when the bow arm is good, the staccato should present no great problem.

ILLUSTRATION 35 Setting the bow hand for the slurred staccato practice.

The Flying Staccato and the Flying Spiccato
(Same marking as solid staccato)

These two strokes are similar to one another, but each has its own individual characteristics. The first of the two, as the name implies, derives from the staccato. It is performed with the same motion as the solid staccato, except that the pressure is lightened and the bow is permitted—and encouraged—to leave the string after each note. This lifting should be only very slight, however, and the movement should remain essentially a horizontal one without interruption in its continual forward flow. This bowing is customarily done on the up-bow, although one can recognize a type of down-bow application of its technique.

To practice the flying staccato it is best to start with a firm up-bow staccato; then, after this motion is well under way, lighten the hand by lifting the elbow and wrist, and add a small amount of vertical finger motion, which will help the bow bounce off the strings after each note. The execution will vary according to the different individual styles of staccato playing. In most cases, the horizontal finger motion will play an important part, with the hand following flexibly and the arm acting in continuous motion. The fingers recover slightly after each individual stroke, in a flexible rebound.

The *flying spiccato* is a succession of spiccato notes on one bow. It may be performed either on the up- or down-bow, but in the latter form it is rather infrequent and is practical only for the succession of a relatively small number of notes. The bow lifts higher than in the flying staccato and, true to its spiccato nature, is actively thrown onto the string for every note. For this reason, its speed is far more limited than that of its staccato counterpart.

Vertical finger motion and vertical hand motion are the main factors in this bowing, with only very little of the horizontal motions mixed in. The smaller the motion, the more it is centered in the fingers; the larger the single strokes, the more prominent the contribution of the hand and even of the arm.

The flying spiccato, too, can be effectively "recovered," staying in one place in the. bow. The recovery serves a double purpose: it permits the uninterrupted use of this bowing even for the longest passages and it helps maintain the same sound-character on the stroke that would otherwise change as the bow varies its point of attack relative to its length. Example 67 gives a good illustration of the "recovered" type.

Example 67
Mendelssohn: *Concerto in E minor*, Op. 64
Finale (measures 129–32)

In the flying spiccato, the strokes can even be made to retrogress, so that in a succession of up-bow spiccatos the bow actually approaches the point. This retrogression is a good practice device, and it occasionally finds its place in actual performance when the need arises to work up toward a higher place in the bow.

Ricochet (Marking: ⌣⌣⌣)

This bowing is based entirely on the natural bounce of the stick. Several notes are played on the same bow, either up or down, but only one impulse is given, that which occurs when the bow is thrown onto the string for the first note. Following this initial impulse, the bow is permitted to jump on its own, not unlike the bouncing of a rubber ball. In this sense the ricochet may be called an "uncontrolled" bowing, in contrast to the flying staccato which, although it utilizes the natural bounce for getting the bow off the strings, actually transmits to each note a separate impulse in the staccato action itself. A still greater contrast exists with the flying spiccato where, for every note, the bow is thrown independently onto the string.

The speed of the ricochet can be regulated, however. Otherwise it would be impractical. The regulation is accomplished by varying the place on the bow and by controlling the height of the bounce. Playable in about the upper two-thirds of the bow, the bounce is faster near the point and progressively slower as the distance from the point increases. Also, it is faster when it does not jump so high and slower when it rebounds farther. The height of the bounce can be regulated by the first impulse and also by an ever-so-slight and delicate pressure of the first finger, which can thereby put a definite ceiling onto the rebound and thus speed it up. For the best rebound, the bow should be held "upright"—with the stick directly above the hair, not tilted.

The ricochet is easier on the down-bow than on the up-bow, and, therefore, practice should start with the down stroke. Begin with two notes a little above the middle of the bow. Let the bow drop without any force from a height of about one inch, and use principally the vertical finger motion and a slight amount of forearm rotation. Let the bow rebound without interfering with the natural bounce, and after the second note stop the motion. Return in the air to the starting point and repeat the process. Continue with three, four, five, six, and more notes, gradually building up the skill as given in Example 68(a). Then do the same exercise, adding an extra note on the end of each group and taking this note up-bow [Example 68(b)]. Finally, reverse the direction, taking the up-bow for the ricochet and the down-bow for the closing note.

Example 68

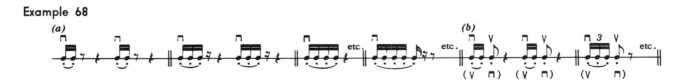

When the exercises given in Example 68 are functioning well, practice the change of strings, as shown in Example 69 (next page).

Example 69

Now take up scales, starting with a few notes and gradually increasing their number.

Examples 70 and 71 present two excerpts of typical ricochet passages. The customary notation of such a bowing is shown in Example 70.

Example 70
Paganini: *24 Caprices*, Op. 1
No. 9 (measures 61–63)

Example 71
Mendelssohn: *Concerto in E minor*, Op. 64
First movement cadenza
(seventh measure of sixteenth notes)

The four note arpeggiated chord is given in Example 71. This instance is the most common form of the ricochet and also the easiest.

Such four-string arpeggios are easy, because the change of strings in itself is helpful to the bounce. The principal impulse is given on the bass note with vertical finger action and vertical hand action. Often, especially in faster tempos, this impulse will carry over into the up-bow, but sometimes a secondary impulse will be needed on the first note of the up-bow. The change of strings is done entirely by the arm, which in faster speeds will move in one smooth and uninterrupted arc.

For practice purposes, it is a good plan to start the arpeggio in the reverse direction: that is, beginning with the E string note and the up-bow. The chief impulse is thus given on the top string, the G string having none, or at most very little (Example 72).

Example 72

Trouble with the ricochet often occurs when one of three things is being done: (1) the bow is being held too tightly, (2) the wrong part of the bow is being used for the speed desired, or (3) the natural bounce is being interfered with because of tenseness in the natural springs.

At the beginning of this section describing the various styles of bowing it was pointed out that the varieties described are only the most characteristic types, from which others can be derived by mixing. Each of these characteristic types has one other (or more) related to it, with which it can be made to blend in a gradual transition. Therefore, after mastering the principal types, the student has to learn the art of gradual, unbroken transition from one to another. First he should concentrate on the patterns which are most closely related such as: (1) legato-portato, (2) any type of détaché to any other type, (3) short martelé to sustained martelé, (4) collé to spiccato, (5) short and fast détaché to sautillé, (6) sautillé to spiccato, (7) solid staccato to flying staccato, (8) spiccato to flying spiccato, and so on. In all of these instances, the order should also be reversed. After this, transitions should be practiced to less closely related patterns similar to the following: (1) détaché to spiccato, (2) martelé to détaché, (3) sautillé to ricochet, (4) portato to staccato, and so on. Scales, arpeggios, or studies like the Kreutzer E major etude (No. 8) will be good media for such practice. In the case of the etudes, alternations of style may occur from measure to measure. A bowing technique cannot be called complete until it has subjugated all of the many and fine transition-shades to its unqualified command.

SPECIAL BOWING PROBLEMS

In order to round out this chapter on bow technique, there is a need to comment on a few special problems. These refer to bow attack, the change of bow stroke, the alternation of fast and slow strokes, and the tonal aspect of harmonics and chords.

Bow Attack

The manner in which a note is started depends upon how the beginning of the tone is intended to sound: (a) very smooth, vowel-like, and not too definite, (b) clearly defined and consonant-like, or (c) more or less strongly accented.

THE VERY SMOOTH, VOWEL-LIKE BEGINNING. For the very smooth start it will generally be best to bring the bow to the string gently from the air when playing in the lower half of the bow. The bow must not drop vertically but must approach the string from an angle that will become smaller in size as more smoothness is desired. In soft dynamics it is advisable to start the motion from a place very near the string and to use very little bow hair for the initial contact.

THE CLEARLY DEFINED CONSONANT-LIKE ATTACK. For an attack that has to be clearly defined without having an accent, the best method will generally be that known as the "*départ.*" This is performed as follows: the bow is placed on the string with the same pressure that will be used for the actual stroke, not more, not less. The note is then attacked with the immediate use of the same speed of stroke that is to be applied throughout the sounding of the tone. The effect will be a distinct, consonant-like articulation.

THE ACCENTED ATTACK. The départ can be transformed gradually into an accent if greater speed of stroke is used immediately after the start than for the rest of the stroke. To this type of speed-accent greater pressure *prior* to the attack may then be added. The result will be a martelé-type of beginning. When, however, greater pressure is used immediately *on* the start instead of before it, in coordination with greater speed of stroke, the effect will be similar to that of the accented détaché. In addition to these on-the-string starts, accents can also be produced very effectively from the air, either by a "whipped" attack (page 69) or by vertical placing of the bow on the strings with the simultaneous "pinching" similar to a martelé.

All of the various attacks described, those from on the string as well as those from the air, can be used in every degree of dynamic and for single notes as well as double stops and chords. The choice of which attack to use should depend only upon musical reasons, upon the sound-effect desired.

There is one thing more to consider. That is: if, at the frog before the initial attack, the bow is suspended in the air from the arm and wrist, the player gains the advantage of getting, in the last decisive instant, the exact feeling of weight and balance of the whole of the bow-arm-hand unit. This last-minute feeling permits a more precise and sensitive coordination of all factors involved in producing, from the start, a tone with exactly the desired quality in dynamic and nuance.

A very important factor in *quality* of the attack is how the vibrato is used. It has to be exactly coordinated with the rapidly changing dynamics and has to increase and decrease in both width and speed in accord with the corresponding increase and decrease of sound volume.

Change of Bow

There are several problems connected with the change of bow (from down to up and vice versa), but the one that is most important concerns the ability to make the change as smooth and as unnoticeable as possible. Many theories have been developed about this particular point. Some methods prescribe the use of the fingers alone, others the hand and wrist, still others the forearm or whole arm. Yet the essence of the matter does *not* lie in the particular muscles or joints that should participate, but instead in two factors: (1) the bow has to slow down shortly before the change, and (2) the pressure has to be lightened, with both of these elements delicately and precisely coordinated. Whether this is done by fingers, hand, or arm is, as a matter of principle, immaterial. The teacher should not try to change a student's well-coordinated and smooth-sounding change of bow, regardless of how it is done. If, on the other hand, the pupil is encumbered with jerky motions that produce rough changes, remedies must be applied. These may take the form of replacing a finger motion or a hand motion by one performed by the whole arm, or, in the case of an arm movement that is too rigid, loosening the stiffened joints and adding flexible hand and finger motions.

The most common fault encountered is a jerking of the sound that occurs whenever the bow is speeded up before the change instead of being properly slowed down. A large pendulum, slowing down slightly before its deliberate, smooth reversal of direction, is a perfect model for a good bow change.

Alternating Fast and Slow Bows

Of the many problems that arise from the almost infinite variety pertaining to the mixing of the bowing types, one stands out as being especially difficult. That is, the alternating of fast and slow bows without losing a well-balanced sound. This was mentioned briefly in the section on Tone Production (page 56). An exercise will now be described that is devised to help overcome this difficulty.

In a passage such as the one given in Example 73, the single note will normally sound louder owing to the much greater speed of bow stroke used in its execution.

This increased speed has to be compensated for by a lightening of pressure if the dynamic is to be uniformly balanced, and this new speed-pressure combination, on the single note, demands a different sounding point on the string, farther away from the bridge.

In such passages we often find that the string "whistles" on the short note. The cause for this is a slow pick-up of the bow and its failure to gain speed fast enough immediately upon starting. The cure is to give either a slight pinch—if the tempo is

Example 73

not too fast—or a little whip at the beginning of the fast note. Either of these tactics will "catch" the string and impart the necessary starting speed, the required pick-up.

In the quoted example, the up-bow must not sound louder than the down-bow, and the bow pressure, consequently, must be lightened on the single note.

To acquire the right technique, the manner of practice shown in Example 74 can be applied to scales and/or many of the standard etudes.

Example 74

Perform Example 74, first using the section of the bow from middle to point, and during the short rest quickly change the sounding point, either by using the horizontal turning motion of the fingers (Illustration 29) or by pushing the whole bow toward the fingerboard in one fast move. This latter move is made by reaching forward with the whole arm so that the bow is displaced parallel to itself, never abandoning the right angle contact with the strings. Immediately after the shift of sounding point, attack the single note with a slight pinch similar to a martelé stroke. Lift the bow off the strings after a few inches and set it again on the strings at its middle point and on the original sounding point. Repeat the same routine for the next set of notes. The exercise should be played later in different parts of the bow as well as with the whole bow. Gradually, the written rest should be shortened, the pinch replaced by a whip, and the lifting of the bow more and more postponed, until finally the contact with the string is only lightened toward the frog rather than being completely removed. This exercise will be still more beneficial if one not only balances the sound, but also exaggeratedly overbalances, playing the legato (slurred) notes very intensely and the single note very lightly during practice.

Harmonics

In many cases where the left-hand work is perfect the harmonics will fail because the bowing is defective. Most commonly, harmonics are attempted with too light a stroke when actually they speak and sound best when played with a *fairly heavy stroke of sufficient length and a sounding point near the bridge.* In double harmonics it will sometimes be necessary to vary the pressure of the bow on the two strings, especially if a mixture of natural and artificial harmonics is involved of which the former needs less pressure than the latter.

Chords

There are three elements involved in the playing of chords. The first two, intonation and what might be called the *building of the chords*, concern the left hand and have been discussed in the chapter devoted to its problems. The third element is the sound production, and it will occupy our attention in the following paragraphs.

Whenever difficulties arise with chords the three elements just mentioned should at first be practiced singly and only thereafter recombined.

As far as the right hand execution is concerned, there are three principal types of chords:

(a) the broken chord in which the lower notes are played before the beat (similar to the execution of a grace note) and the upper notes arrive *on* the beat;

(b) the unbroken chord in which either all notes are played simultaneously, or the lower notes are attacked *on* the beat with the higher ones coming imperceptibly later;

(c) the turned chord, used mainly in polyphonic music and played in such a way that a note other than the top note emerges at the end of the chord.

BROKEN CHORDS. If a three-note chord is broken, the usual procedure is to attack the low and middle notes together before the beat and then to move over to the highest note in such a way that the middle and high note are sounded together exactly on the beat (Example 75).

The middle string acts as a pivot and is sounded throughout. It is advisable to put some extra pressure on the middle string during pivoting, because this reduces the angle of the breaking motion as the bow moves from the string-level of the two lower notes to that of the two higher notes. Greater smoothness is thereby achieved.

Other less-used ways of breaking the three-note chord are shown in Example 76.

Four-note chords can also be broken in various ways. The most frequent style is shown in Example 77.

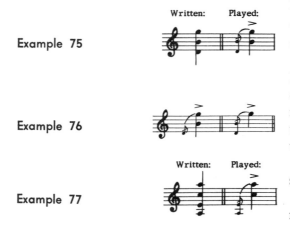

Example 75

Example 76

Example 77

In Example 77 the bow attacks the G and D strings together shortly before the beat and then turns over to the A and E strings exactly on the beat. This is the pertinent execution when the top notes have to be emphasized. If smoothness rather than accentuation is wanted, then the breaking will assume more of an arpeggio character, will be more rolled than broken. The depicting of such an execution is approximated in "slow-motion" notation in Example 78.

If, in four-note chords, all notes are fingered, it is sometimes advisable to lift the fingers off the G and D strings after they have sounded in order to give the hand more freedom to vibrate the upper notes. Conversely, if it is more desirable to keep an after-ring on the bass notes, the fingers must be kept down on the strings, since the vibration stops immediately when they are lifted.

Some of the other possibilities of breaking four-note chords are shown in Example 79.

The action involved in the breaking of chords is chiefly centered in a downward motion of the whole arm together with a supination of the forearm as the crossing is made. The elbow drops slightly before the actual breaking of the chord (all of this in addition, of course, to the movements necessary for the common bow stroke).

A high elbow is especially disadvantageous to chord playing, since it prevents the utilization of much of the weight of the arm, which weight is, unfortunately, being carried in the air by muscular effort rather than being allowed to add to the volume of sound. A high elbow also makes it almost impossible to keep the bow straight.

It will most often be best not to attack the broken chord from a position *on* the string but instead to drop the bow from the air. In doing so, all of the springs of the arm, hand and fingers will have to work well, especially those of the vertical finger and hand motions.

UNBROKEN CHORDS. Unbroken chords of three notes, when attacked simultaneously, can either be sustained throughout, as shown in Example 80, or else, after the simultaneous attack, only one or two notes held out, as in Example 81.

Example 78

Example 79

Example 80
Paganini: *24 Caprices*, Op. 1
No. 24: variation 8, beginning

Example 81
Bach: *Sonata No. 1 in G minor*
Second Movement: Fugue (measures 30–31)

The best way to produce the simultaneous attack of the three-note chord is to suspend the bow slightly above the middle string, then to drop it straight down for a good solid grip on the strings. Pressure has to be sufficiently great to depress the middle string far enough for the neighboring strings to be properly contacted and sounded by the bow. Such an attack from the air will almost always be preferable to one starting on the strings. It will save bow, since the drop will provide energy that has otherwise to be gained in horizontal attack. (Moreover, the previously mentioned advantage won by the exact feeling of the weight-balance factors of the bow, hand, and arm will be especially valuable with such a simultaneous chord-attack in which the slightest miscalculation can lead to tonal failure.)

The movement is performed by the whole arm, but the dropping must be made with flexible (though not too loose) springs and must land on a well-chosen sounding point. Furthermore, this drop has to be vertical for the simultaneous attack. If the bow should approach the strings in too horizontal a line, the attack will be less precise, less clear, and less forceful, owing to the poorly used weight factor.

Chords of simultaneous attack, especially when sustained, are much easier for the bow if it plays somewhat nearer the fingerboard rather than near the bridge, but for anything other than a piano dynamic the position near the fingerboard will rarely be satisfactory. In louder dynamics, therefore, the solution will be a compromise between the desirability of playing the chord near the bridge and the difficulty of doing so without crushing the sound of the middle note, which can happen when playing closer to the curvature of the bridge where the strings have little "give."

Most violinists play chords always at the frog of the bow. Yet often a too heavy attack at the frog will cause a scratchy sound. One has to learn to play chords in any part of the bow, using up-bow as well as down. In softer dynamics particularly, a place in the middle or even in the upper half of the bow will sometimes be advisable. A good illustration is offered by the example from the A minor Fugue of Bach (Example 82). If it is played in piano, the chords will best be taken in the middle of the bow.

TURNED CHORDS. Chords in polyphonic music present a special problem, because they have to be played in a way that not only does not interrupt the continuity of the individual voices but also actually helps to clarify their individual sequences. This means in particular (1) that the chords should have fullness and resonance without unnecessary accents and (2) that the notes

Example 82
Bach: *Sonata No. 2 in A minor*
Second movement: Fugue (measures 151–52)

belonging to the independent voices must be well sustained after the chord is sounded as a whole.

If the melody note is on the top, or is second from the top, there is little difficulty. In the first instance, all that has to be done is to sustain the top note longer than the second highest note, so that its meaning as melody note is emphasized (Example 83).

Example 83
Bach: *Sonata No. 1 in G minor*
First movement (last two measures)

The same is true when the second highest note is the melody note. It then has to be held out longer than the top note as is shown in both chords in Example 84.

When the melody note is the third note from the top in a three-note chord that can be attacked simultaneously, it is still fairly simple: after attacking all three strings together, the two upper strings are released and only the lowest note continues to be bowed (Example 85).

The technical process involved centers around the element of pronation plus a slight lifting of the upper arm, both of which are added to the motion of the chord attack.

Sometimes, however, the simultaneous attack will not be appropriate; this is especially true when the nature of the voice leading requires a turning of the chord from above. In Example 86, for instance, the indicated method of execution is the only one that will clarify how one phrase ends and the other one starts.

In four-note chords with the melody on the D string (Example 87, next page) it is preferable to do the turning of the chord in such a way that the melody note on the D string, which is attacked on the beat, can be kept sounding throughout, the bow not losing contact therewith at any time. Such a rendition is shown as (a) in the example.

This, however, involves a great amount of pressure in order to sound three strings simultaneously. If this cannot be done without undue accent, then the method under (b) should be applied; but in this latter case one must try to keep the D string sounding as long as possible so that the reiteration is barely noticeable. The actual turning to the upper string and return should be done very rapidly.

Example 84
Bach: *Sonata No. 1 in G minor*
First movement (measure 2)

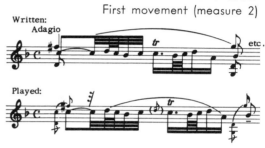

Example 85
Bach: *Sonata No. 1 in G minor*
Second movement: Fugue (measures 20–21)

Example 86
Bach: *Sonata No. 1 in G minor*
Third movement: Siciliana (measure 4)

Example 87
Bach: *Partita No. 2 in D minor*
Chaconne (measure 10)

Example 88
Bach: *Sonata No. 2 in A minor*
Second movement: Fugue (measures 40–41)

Four-note chords with the melody in the bass are currently being rendered in many different ways, such as, for example, those shown under Example 88.

Any of these styles will find a proper place in a certain pertinent context, but none of these can be considered an ideal solution *as a standard procedure*, especially in a succession of chords. When such passages occur, the best solution of the problem is to anticipate the melodic note with an accent *preceding* the beat and then to play the rest of the chord in the usual way, taking care, however, that the bass is louder than the other three notes. This procedure is approximated in notation as given in Example 89.

If the finger for the lowest note is left in position on the string and keeps vibrating, a pedal effect will be achieved, and the bass note will continue to ring after the bow has left it. Played in this way, not only will the melody stand out sufficiently but the other voices will also be brought into far better relief than is possible with any of the other methods.

Sometimes a particular type of voice leading will be best projected by mixing the various styles of chord execution. The original notation of a pertinent passage is given in Example 90(a), with the suggested execution notated under (b).

Example 89

Example 90
Bach: *Sonata No. 3 in C major*
Second movement: Fugue (measures 56–58)

Chapter Four
ON PRACTICING

T HE ROAD TO VIOLIN MASTERY is long and arduous, and great application and perseverance are needed to reach the goal. Talent helps to ease the way, but in itself it cannot be a substitute for the hard work of practicing. Even hard work will be of little avail if it is of the kind that fails to bring results, for there are both good practicing and bad practicing, and unfortunately the bad is far more common than the good.

There is nothing more precious to an instrumentalist than the ability to work efficiently—to know how to accomplish the maximum in beneficial results while using the minimum of time to do so. One of the most important things that a teacher ought to teach his students is, therefore, the technique of good practice. He has to impress on his students that practice has to be a continuation of the lesson, that it is nothing but a process of self-instruction in which, in the absence of the teacher, the student has to act as the teacher's deputy, assigning himself definite tasks and supervising his own work. A teacher who limits himself to pointing out the mistakes and does not show the proper way to overcome them fails in the important mission of teaching the student how to work for himself.

MENTAL ALERTNESS IN PRACTICE

The thing that must be impressed on the student above all else is the necessity for complete and constant mental alertness during practice. It happens only too often with too many students that the mind wanders to different spheres while the fingers and hands are engaged in mechanical routine-functioning and endless repetitions. Practice of this kind, lacking both direction and control, is a waste of time and effort. Not only does it not achieve what it sets out to do, but also it can sometimes be positively harmful. Mistakes are repeated over and over again, and the ear becomes impervious to faulty sounds. Whenever such a type of practicing (where mind and ear are not on the job) has become a deeply rooted habit, a great effort of the will must be made to make the mind and ear become completely and constantly alert. Where insufficient attention is due only to a state of tiredness, all that is needed as a cure is a different organization of practice time and material—a change, so to speak, in the practice hygiene. General rules in this respect cannot be well formulated.

It does not make sense to demand dogmatically that every student should practice a certain number of hours according to a certain rigid schedule. Requirements and possibilities will vary greatly in individual cases: one student can remain fresh longer than another; and besides, not every student is free to organize his day solely around his violin practice. All that can be stated in a generalization is that individually the student has to find out by intelligent experimenting what is best for himself. He should not, however, become inflexible by rigidly sticking to the same routine. There is no necessity to have a set pattern for the *sequence* of practice material, for example, scales first, then etudes, then repertoire. There is no reason why this order should not be modified and practice started with pieces and ended with scales as long as all of the work is done that should be accomplished. Mixing the material and not dwelling too long on a single item will often help to keep the mind fresh longer. It is important, of course, that the practice time is utilized well throughout, and that practicing becomes a daily habit. Regular, daily practice will put the student much farther ahead than will long, intense periods irregularly and spasmodically spaced.

THE OBJECTIVES IN PRACTICE

Both technique and interpretation have to be objectives in practicing. The shape and coloring of a phrase has to be worked.

It is very important to have an intelligently balanced division of practice hours, distributed between (1) "building time" (devoted to overcoming technical problems and advancing one's equipment in general), and (2) "interpreting time" (devoted to making the playing of a musical work conform to one's own interpretive ideas). A (3) "performing time" should be added whenever a piece is being readied for actual performance. During this performing time a whole composition is played without stops and preferably with accompaniment, bearing in mind the idea that imaginary listeners are present.

The "Building Time"

The building time should be spent partly with scales and similar fundamental exercises and partly in dealing with technical problems encountered in etudes and in the repertoire.

For all types of technical practice, the principle of *mental preparation* is of paramount importance. It means that the mind always has to anticipate the physical action that is to be taken and then to send the command for its execution. This, it will be remembered, is what I have called "correlation." It is the key to technical control, and all practice concerned with the building of technique or the overcoming of particular difficulties has to center on the development and improvement of this correlation. The way to do this was briefly indicated previously, but now it is time to be more specific and to give some examples that will clarify the subject.

The basic procedure is to present to the mind, for transmission to the muscles, problems that progress from the simple to the ever more complicated. These are problems of timing and coordination in the form of various patterns of rhythm, of bowing, of accentuation, and of the combination of all three of these factors.

In progressing from simpler to harder problems one very important principle has to be kept in mind, a principle that applies to any type of practicing: whenever one problem is mastered, it is useless to repeat it over and over again. One should leave it alone and proceed to the next. By practicing, as a routine, things that do not need any more practice, one is wasting time. There is no objection, of course, to returning after a certain interval of time in order to check on whether the possessed skill is still secure or whether any repairs are due. For the most part, however, the guiding idea must be to solve one problem and then to proceed to the next one.

Example 91 presents the basic outline for the improvement of correlation and coordination.

Example 91: The Scale Routines

In the following set of routines, Section IV, dealing with the mixture of slurs and separate bows, stresses the coordination of the two hands. In slow practice, the separate bows are martelé, in faster practice they become détaché. Intelligent thought must be given to solving the problems of even distribution of bow wherever possible and to the application of more of the weight-pressure factors on the slurs where the even distribution is not possible. Section V deals with accentuation. When all of the problems presented here are solved and have become efficient parts of the over-all technique, then the student should build new problems for himself, finding new rhythmical combinations and uniting into one problem several of the given examples. Such might be, for instance, the first rhythm of Section II followed immediately by the second rhythm in sequence and alternating; or, in still more advanced stages, the third, fourth, fifth and/or sixth bowings of Section II in conjunction with the accentuation patterns of Section V. As was said before, the combinations are infinite and when the student has mastered any one routine he should proceed to the next.

The A-major scale, 24-note version

Section 1: Slurs

Section 2: Rhythms (slur 12 notes)

The following groupings are to be practiced in both (a) and (b) forms as given in the example immediately preceding.

2 + 6 + 4	2̣ + 6̲ + 4̲
4 + 2 + 6	4̲ + 2̣ + 6̲
4 + 6 + 2	4̲ + 6̲ + 2̣
6 + 2 + 4	6̲ + 2̣ + 4̲
6 + 4 + 2	6̲ + 4̲ + 2̣
1 + 3 + 8	1̣ + 3̲ + 8̲
1 + 8 + 3	1̣ + 8̲ + 3̲
3 + 1 + 8	3̲ + 1̣ + 8̲
3 + 8 + 1	3̲ + 8̲ + 1̣
8 + 1 + 3	8̲ + 1̣ + 3̲
8 + 3 + 1	8̲ + 3̲ + 1̣

Section 3: Slurred Staccatos

Section 4: Bowing patterns

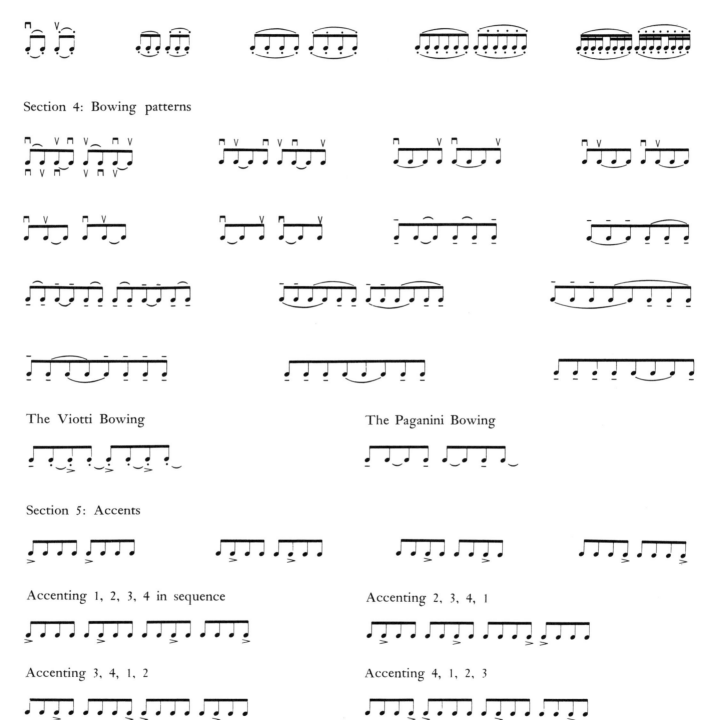

The Viotti Bowing

The Paganini Bowing

Section 5: Accents

Accenting 1, 2, 3, 4 in sequence

Accenting 2, 3, 4, 1

Accenting 3, 4, 1, 2

Accenting 4, 1, 2, 3

The A major scale is used here as an illustration for these procedures, but this type of practice must not be limited to it alone. Such practice should be applied to all work of a "building" nature: scales and arpeggios in all keys, etudes, and the practice of difficult passages in the repertoire.

With this introduction to the method of solving the problems of correlation and coordination, the reader should understand that the combinations given are by no means complete or exhaustive. The number of possibilities is infinite and cannot be covered in a single lifetime. The goal is not merely to play all of the possible combinations, but rather to master a few new ones each day so as to improve and to perfect gradually the coordination and correlation.

Whenever technical problems are encountered, they must be analyzed to determine the nature of the difficulty: intonation, shifting, rhythm, speed, a particular bowing, the coordination of the hands, and so on, or a combination of several of these. Each difficulty should be isolated and reduced to its simplest terms so that it will be easier to devise and to apply a practice procedure for it. The mind, which has to be able to anticipate the action, must have a clear picture of the motion involved, of its technical timing, and of the anticipated sound in order to give its commands with clarity and precision. Practice tempos should be slow, for the most part, but without exaggeration. The problems encountered should be handled by varying the practice devices, by changing the rhythms, bowing, accents, tempos, just as is done in the correlation exercises of Example 91. In this manner one manages to get at the core of the difficulty, not from only one direction, but from many different directions. In this way a higher degree of security can be obtained.

If, for instance, the passage (Example 92) from the Mendelssohn Violin Concerto is to be practiced, all of the various correlation patterns that have been listed will prove of the greatest usefulness in mastering these difficult measures.

Example 92
Mendelssohn: *Concerto in E minor,* Op. 64
First movement (measures 182–84)

The "Interpreting Time"

During the interpreting time the emphasis should be placed on musical expressiveness, the shaping of a phrase, of a larger section, of a whole movement, and finally of several movements, as a convincing unit. Whereas during building time one should never permit a mistake to go uncorrected, during practice for interpretation (and still more so during performing time) it is advisable not to interrupt the execution every time a note is missed or some other small accident occurs. Students who are by nature overly analytical will be especially inclined to stop whenever anything happens that is not to their liking. It is a dangerous habit to form, and it can become treacherous in public performance. Such players will either stop in a concert after making a mistake or will be so upset by it that the rest of the performance is jeopardized. The performer has to command all of his will power to play as well as he can. Above all else he must not let himself be unnerved if anything goes wrong. One way to learn this skill is to break the interruption habit in the practice room during the performing time.

If necessary, the teacher must train the student in this respect, first by making him play sizable sections and then whole movements, forbidding him to stop unless instructed to do so by the teacher. Even if a major mistake is made the student must learn to extricate himself from the difficult situation and to catch the beat again as soon as and as best he can. Obviously, it is an excellent idea to remember the things that did go wrong so that they can be corrected.

An incorrect balance of building and interpreting time will lead to other faulty practice habits. Some players neglect the building time and concertize for themselves during most of their working hours. They may develop a good feeling for the musical continuity of a work, but its difficult passages will continue unmastered and the technical equipment in general will remain deficient. On the other extreme, there are students who know only "building time." They break up every measure, even the simplest, into its component elements and keep working with those elements without ever putting them together again. For such students a composition ceases to be a living work of art, but remains forever a series of technical challenges. By being so absorbed in details they fail ever to get the feeling of the piece as a whole.

Each of these extremes needs a healthy counterweight in order to restore the proper balance of interpreting and building time. The "concertizer" must spend more time in analyzing his mistakes and in devising and applying remedies to overcome them. The over-analytical student should assign much more time to musical playing, in small as well as large units, putting together that which he has pulled apart.

The "Performing Time"

The necessity for adding musical playing to analytical dissection of difficulties is well demonstrated by a phenomenon that can be observed time and time again. A student practices a difficult passage from a piece. He analyzes it properly, transforms it into well-devised exercises, and finally masters it technically. Yet when he plays the whole piece this same passage fails to come off properly and sometimes even breaks down completely. How can this be explained? The answer lies in the entirely different conditions of mind and muscles in the playing of a passage as an exercise and in playing it as part of a musical composition. In the complete rendition, the addition of vibrato, the concern for expression, for nuance and dynamics, all add entirely new elements that were not present when the passage was segregated for the cold technical study. These additional factors disturb the smooth functioning of the practiced passage. This is not the fault of the mechanical approach, which is still the indispensable first step in overcoming technical difficulties in pieces. What has been overlooked is the fact that after this first step has been taken and the passage has been mastered from a purely technical point of view, *it must be practiced again as a piece of music*, in the context of a larger section and with the expression that is its due. Only then has one a right to expect that the isolated section can be successfully integrated again into the piece and made to grow together with the rest of the work without showing a seam or a scar.

THE CRITICAL EAR

In whatever type of practice one is engaged—technical difficulties of either hand, tone quality, interpretation—the mental preparation and control has to be supplemented by the sharpest and most constant supervision by the critical ear. The *sound* produced has to be under permanent scrutiny. The ear is always the final judge in deciding what is good and what is not. With most players, however, the ear is defective in fulfilling this function. They do not know how to listen to hear the sound actually produced: they do not hear *objectively*. Instead, they hear *subjectively*. The things they actually hear are strongly distorted by what they want and hope to hear. When they have an opportunity to make a recording they are shocked to find things they would never believe they had actually done. To train the ear for objective listening is of the greatest importance in order to be able to hear the sound as the audience would hear it and to free oneself from the flattering fallacies of the subjective ear. The ability for honest, objective hearing is the most essential prerequisite for efficient practice.

BASIC EXERCISES

Before leaving this chapter on practicing, I must make a few remarks concerning some basic exercises for both the left and right hands.

Scales

The scales have been studied ever since the violin has been played. Their great importance lies in the fact that they can serve as a vehicle for the development of a large number of technical skills in either the left or right hand. Scales build intonation and establish the frame of the hand; their usefulness for the practice of correlation was discussed; their applicability for the study of all bowings, of tone quality, of bow division, of dynamics, and of vibrato is almost endless.

When the scales are practiced as single notes (not double stops) they should first be learned with a definite fingering pattern, starting from the tonic. Next, different fingerings should be applied. Finally, the scale should be started on notes other than the tonic. This is another way of saying that each scale may be practiced with many different signatures.

Scales in double stops follow a similar pattern. As a preparation for such double stops, it is a good device to finger both notes simultaneously while bowing only one of the two strings involved.

In most of the double stop scales the fingering may be changed after the basic pattern is learned: where odd-numbered positions have been used, for example, even-numbered ones should be substituted, and vice versa.

Scales in double stops should also be played in various rhythms, bowings, and accentuations. At first, however, fewer notes should be taken on one bow than with the single note scales. Later the number of notes can be gradually increased.

Arpeggios in single notes as well as double stops should be practiced also in the same manner. In single note arpeggios especially, changes of fingering should be applied after the basic type has been mastered.

The Son Filé

Probably as old as the study of scales is the practicing of the *son filé*, namely, the long sustained tone, which has served generations of violinists as a medium for the study of tone production and bow control, and which still provides valuable exercise material for the same purpose. What breath control is for the singer—the ability to sing long phrases without having to interrupt them for a new breath—bow control in the long, sustained stroke is for the violinist—the ability to sustain a long tone or musical phrase without having to change bow.

The *son filé* should be practiced on open strings, then on scales singly and in double stops: in every dynamic from piano to forte and with dynamic variations as shown in Example 93.

Example 93

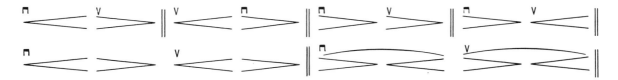

The idea is to hold back the bow stroke as much as possible without interrupting the continuity of sound. Starting at a certain slow speed, one should aim at being able to play slower and slower. The ear has to supervise the quality of the sound produced, its resonance, and its evenness. It is aided, in getting results from this supervisory task, by the fingers of the right hand, especially the index finger, which has to be educated to the sensitivity of feeling the resistance of the strings and thereby of gaging the pressure and friction exerted by the bow on the strings.

Important as the *son filé* is for the development of bow control and tone production, exercises combining long bows with frequent changes of notes (slurred) as well as changes of strings, are still more advantageous. Especially in cases where the player has a tendency to stiffening, the wavelike movements connected with the change of strings will have a definite loosening effect on the rigidity of the wrist and hand. Exercises like the Kreutzer Nos. 14 and 29, the Wieniawski Opus 10, No. 7, and similar studies lend themselves well to such practice. As skill is developed, the tempo is slowed down, thus requiring still more sustaining control from the bow.

"Spring" Exercises

Another set of practice patterns based on the skills of tone production are those that could be called the "spring" exercises. They are designed to improve the working of the natural springs (page 44). Their goal is to help the student to get the deepest, fullest sound without forcing, and to be conscious of the working of each spring.

THE ROULÉ. The first of these exercises, the Roulé, has been suggested by Capet. It consists of playing a sustained note on either a single tone or a double stop and rolling the bow between the fingers during the stroke so that the stick will lean alternately toward the fingerboard and toward the bridge. This rolling of the stick should be done gradually and smoothly, without jerking, and the sound should be kept as full, round, and even as possible. The symbols (Example 94) denote the changing angle of the bow-stick as it rotates around the hair as an axis.

Example 94
(After Capet)

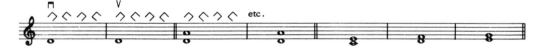

⟨ stick rolled toward fingerboard
⟨ stick rolled toward the bridge

Lucien Capet LA TECHNIQUE SUPÉRIEURE DE L'ARCHET (Paris, Editions Maurice Senart 1916, rev. 1929) pp. 24–25. By permission of Editions Salabert, 22 rue Chauchat, Paris, France.

FLEXIBILITY OF THE SPRINGS IN THE WRIST AND FOREARM. A second exercise consists essentially of a rotary motion of the forearm (page 50) at the frog, gradually passing to the vertical motion of the hand (Illustration 31) as the bow moves downward toward the point. This is an undulating motion which should be practiced, preferably, using double stops.

After the foregoing exercises are well assimilated, they should be taken up again from time to time, especially whenever any kind of stiffness develops in the right arm.

Conclusion

A FEW WORDS
FOR THE TEACHER

IN ADDRESSING, BY WAY OF CONCLUSION, a few remarks to the
teacher, I have first to revert to what I said at the very beginning of this book, i.e., that students are not alike and should not
be treated alike, and that teaching according to rigid rules is
teaching of the wrong kind. The teacher who takes his mission
seriously will see in every single student an entirely new and
challenging problem. At first the teacher has to study the student to get a clear picture of his playing, his musicianship, his
personality. As to the playing, the teacher must discover both
weaknesses and strengths. He must judge the potentialities of
the student and decide whether there are hindrances in the way
of their development; whether there are bad habits involved or
dangerous tendencies present. Such things as weak fingers or
joints must be noticed. In judging bad habits, the teacher must
know enough and be broad-minded enough not to classify as
bad habits everything that does not conform exactly to his own
personal way of playing. The teacher should not look for devia-
tions from rules but should try to find out whether there is any
real handicap present that needs to be removed.

Once the teacher has made the diagnosis of the student's playing, he should know what needs to be done: where hindrances
exist that have to be cleared away, where he can start building,
which aspects of the playing are underdeveloped and need
greater care or emphasis than others.

The decision of how and when to do all of these things, however, will have to be based on a considered judgment of the student's personality. This is why it is so important that the attitude of the teacher be a very personal one and, of concomitant importance, that he analyze the character of every student correctly. It can take weeks—sometimes months—but once the teacher has gained the necessary knowledge, he can proceed with the greatest assurance in planning the special kind of treatment that will bring with it the greatest and fastest results.

The teacher must be a good psychologist. He must beware of discouraging the student, and he must know that there are times when it is advisable to correct certain things and times when it is not advisable to do so. In the latter case, he must postpone the corrections until the propitious moment arrives. He must be able to judge, in such cases, what is important at the moment and must be taken care of right away, and what can wait for later. Above all, the teacher must not try to do too much at once. The ability to digest new things is limited with everybody, and an over-ambitious attempt on the part of the teacher to apply too many cures simultaneously will yield negative results.

Encouragement of the student and the building of self-confidence are also matters that must be thoughtfully planned. The teacher should sense in each case when it is necessary to give moral support by encouragement and praise, and when to resort to strictness and censure. Some students, especially the conscientious and shy types, prosper when given a great deal of praise and encouragement. This same treatment, applied to certain other students, can be very harmful, causing them to relax their efforts. To build self-confidence too soon can be almost as dangerous as not to build it at all. Strict treatment works well with some pupils, but it is dangerous for others.

Whatever the teacher does, whatever kind of treatment he metes out, he must do it with a cool head and as a planned tactic. Should he decide, for example, that a certain student would be greatly benefited by a scolding he should give it to him according to plan. This is an entirely different matter from doing the same thing in a fit of temper—which should never happen in the teacher-student relationship.

The teacher should know that every student passes through recurring stages of varying response. He should try to guess the periods of special productivity and try to take the best possible advantage of them.

In teaching as well as in practicing there has to be a balance between "building" and "interpreting." To emphasize only the interpretive element will result in neglect of technical equipment, while an exclusive concern with the technical factors will cripple the imagination as well as the ability for spontaneous music-making. The balance between these two factors will have to differ in various stages of the student's development. In the early years, the teacher should see his prime duty as the building of an instrumental equipment. He should not neglect the *musical* growth, but the building factor should be in the foreground. *There is no age limit for the development of musicianship, but early youth is the time when technique grows fastest.* At a later stage, when the technique is solidly built on secure foundations, the balance can then shift more toward the interpretive element.

Concerning this interpretive side of teaching, it was pointed out much earlier in this work that the teacher makes a grave mistake when he insists on imposing on the student his own individual musical version of every piece. Instead, the teacher should encourage and inspire the advanced pupils to an independent and personal rendition, guiding it when necessary in such a way that it will conform to the aesthetic dictates of good taste, style, and form. Here, as in every other respect too, the prime duty of the teacher is to educate the student to stand on his own feet, musically as well as technically.

As to the choice of material to be used in teaching, no specific plan can be given, because it all has to be adapted to individual needs. The importance of scales and allied exercises for the building of every element of technique, and especially of *correlation*, has already been stressed. Etudes are very important, too, because they build technique that functions in a musical setting, and many of the standard etude works may be used to advantage.

Concerning repertoire, the teacher should aim at giving the greatest possible variety and versatility and at having the student cover works of all styles, types, and periods. Teachers should not take the line of least resistance by giving the student only those pieces for which he is most naturally adapted. The repertoire should be well rounded for all students in order that any one-sided development may be avoided.

For study purposes, the weakest points should be given special attention. For public performance, however, it will be wiser to choose a program that is best suited to the personality of the student and will show his special talents to the best advantage.

That the teacher himself should have a thorough knowledge of the instrument is a matter of course. Also, his horizon should not be limited to the violin repertoire. If it is, his interpretive and musical guidance will leave much to be desired.

The teacher should be conscientious, patient, and even-tempered. Above all, he must have real love and enthusiasm for his work. Good teaching takes a measure of devotion that the teacher is unable to give unless his heart and soul are dedicated to it.

Postscript
GALAMIAN IN THE STUDIO

Elizabeth A. H. Green

I. THE INTRODUCTION
TO THE GALAMIAN METHOD

> Most powerful is he who has himself in his own power.
> SENECA

A small plaque inscribed with Seneca's words hung unobtrusively on the wall inside the kitchen door at Meadowmount, the summer violin school for the Galamian students. Mr. Galamian himself radiated that kind of power. One felt it even the first time one met him. He inspired confidence, was most courteous, and was, in the present day vernacular, "unflappable."

Tall and thin, Mr. Galamian carried himself with a certain confident authority, and his Armenian facial features were vitalized by his great dark eyes that could be stern, if necessary, or could sparkle with spontaneous laughter. His penetrating gaze studied the student throughout the lesson and, truly, nothing escaped him.

As students, we were taught, also, to get ourselves under control—an absolute technical control. Our teacher woke us up to the mental power most of us used only casually. His practice assignments were such that we could not accomplish them with success unless the mind was working constantly and in-

tently. ("The mind learns through the solving of problems.")
When we used his practice methods there was no way we could
avoid thinking.

Our first discovery was that, with Mr. Galamian, an etude
was not just one more study to be learned. It became, instead, a
panorama of pertinent technique. Various rhythms for the left
hand were superimposed, as were diverse bowings, so that the
mind was working constantly during the practice hours. Mr.
Galamian called these innovations "problems for the mind to
solve." They were oriented to the basic content of the study,
beginning in each etude with something less difficult and becoming steadily more demanding, often combining new left-
hand rhythms with expanded bowing techniques. By the end
of the practice week we found ourselves doing things, mentally
and physically, we could only have stumbled over when the
week began. Our whole level of performance had subtly moved
ahead a pace. Mr. Galamian often remarked, "As a teacher, my
first task is to teach the students *how* to practice. Once they
understand this, they begin to make progress."

When the individual "problems" (or variations) were mastered, they were often combined in fast, uninterrupted sequence, measure by measure, motif by motif. The mind was
challenged to think with tremendous speed and an even greater
degree of concentration. "What is of paramount importance is
not the physical movements as such but the mental control over
them" (Introduction, page 2).

Visitors who spent a day at Meadowmount, perhaps auditing
a lesson or two, saw a session very similar to what may occur
in any fine studio. They went away with the mystery still un-
solved: *But how does he do it?* The answer to their astonished
query lay not in what they saw but in what they could not see:
namely, in what was going on in the student's mind during the
brilliant performance. The manner in which the mental-physical
response had been systematically and carefully nurtured during
the weeks of study was not visible. Only the student knew that
what went through his or her mind, musically, imaginatively,
would come out easily and effortlessly in the ultimate performance.

In the forties and fifties, our instruction began with "The
A-Major Scale" (pages 96–98). Later on, after the scale method
was published, Mr. Galamian used the G-major scale. Was there
ever a Galamian student who escaped the scales? (As I left my
first lesson, a little twelve-year-old tot came bouncing up. Said
she, "Well what did you get? The A-major scale?")

It was a source of quiet amusement with the students of
longer standing as they secretly watched the new student take
the first lesson and "get the A-major scale." But the amusement

was always tempered with the knowledge that very soon the new student would come to realize that our genius of a teacher had introduced us, in that very first lesson, to a whole new way to conquer troublesome technical passages. The rhythms and bowings of the A-major scale were to be used in a practical way. There was an ever-present element of discovery as we found ourselves building technique in excess of what a passage actually required. The original notation thereafter became easy to execute and, concomitantly, our whole technique was improving.

"There is nothing more precious to an instrumentalist than the ability to work effectively—to know how to accomplish the maximum of beneficial results using the minimum of time to do so" (page 93). Yes, nothing succeeds like success!

Mr. Galamian showed supreme artistry when it came to building ease of physical performance for each student. He was always aware of the student as a person. "The teacher must realize that every student is an individual with his own personality, his own characteristic physical and mental make-up, his own approach to the instrument and to music" (page 1). "The teacher should be prepared to deal with such differences . . . by making compromises to fit the particular student" (page 2).

Physically, attention was focused on certain things. First, an unshrugged bow-arm shoulder. "Raising (shrugging) the shoulder . . . *has no place at all* in a sound bowing technique. . . . It is the evil source of frustrations and disturbances in the bow arm" (page 51). In the studio, if Mr. Galamian saw the student's shoulder begin to pull up, he would tap it gently, reminding the pupil to relax the tension. As shrugging was eliminated, ease of motion was acquired.

Bowing

The approach to the bow stroke was unique. Mr. Galamian understood that any bending or opening of the arm *at the elbow* would produce a resultant circular (arclike) motion in the lower arm. Therefore the so-called "straight" bow stroke terminology is not completely accurate, relative to the motion needed for its execution. The mind is thinking "straight" when the arm is necessarily working in curved motions. The awkward terminology concerns the stroke from the middle to the point of the bow. "The mind, which has to be able to anticipate the action, must have a clear picture of the motion involved" (page 97).

The motion can be described as follows: As the arm opens outward, horizontally from the bent elbow, the lower arm will *naturally* swing in a backward-curving arc. If the bow is to retain its right angle relation to the string, this curve has to be gradually canceled by a corresponding forward curve. "This motion [the forward curve] is performed by stretching the forearm and pushing forward with the upper arm" (page 53). The up-bow is simply a reversal of this procedure, that is, the forward reach is gradually retracted. Mr. Galamian called the forward-backward curves the "out-in" motion: "out," down-bow, forward; "in," up-bow, retracting. His term "direction" identified the whole process.

The amount of out-in compensation needed is entirely dependent upon the length of the individual student's arm. The very long arm may not need to adjust until the last inch or so at the point of the bow (see pages 52 and 53). The proper mental concept of what actually occurs in the stroke, coupled with a relaxed bow-arm shoulder, contributes to the ease of the bow-arm's motion. Ideally, the bow retains its right-angle relationship to the string all the way to the tip. *This is the most important single factor in maintaining a clear and sustained tone at the point of the bow and during the bow change.* In the studio, if the student's bow began to go crooked, Mr. Galamian would quietly signal the out-in motion by a gesture of his hand, without interrupting the performance.

The out-in motion was the basic stroke—the fundamental instruction. Later it was tempered with the "slightly slanted stroke" (page 61). The student was made to be constantly attentive to the *quality* of sound produced.

During the first lesson, in addition to the A-major scale and the refining of the bow-stroke, Mr. Galamian would prescribe a large dose of martelé. Here is where he unlocked all of the muscles of the right hand. (Many of us felt that we worked harder with our bow fingers, during those first few weeks, than we did with the fingers of our left hand!) The bow-hand position (Illustration 22) and the finger motions of Illustrations 27, 28, and 29, were all put to work in the initial martelé and collé exercises. (To correct a faulty bow-hand position—little finger stiffly extended—the curative was temporarily to reach the ring finger well over the pearl dot on the far side of the frog. This forced the little finger to curve properly in contacting the stick.)

The martelé is essentially a fast stroke, wherein the "preparation" and "release" are of paramount importance. To produce a martelé that was acceptable to Mr. Galamian took some good, serious, intensive practice. We shall now proceed with a step-wise approach to this stroke.

1. Starting down-bow at the frog, the fingers and thumb are

in the curved position (Illustration 22) and the bow is suspended slightly above the string.

2. To set the bow silently on the string, a very slight vertical finger motion is used (Illustration 27), the fingers and thumb retaining their curved position.

3. For the martelé, the bow "catches" or "pinches" the string upon initiating the stroke. When the stroke begins farther from the frog, pressure is applied by a slight pronation of the arm, lending weight to the first finger on the bow (page 50).

4. In the martelé, a small amount of pressure must be released instantly after the attack. This is accomplished by the motion shown in Illustration 28, page 48. On the down-bow, as the arm initiates the stroke, the thumb and fingers move simultaneously from the curved position to the elongated position (Illustration 28, lower hand). On the up-bow martelé, the motion is from elongated position to curved.

NOTE: When the fingers become active in the curved to elongated position, there is a tendency for the little finger to slip off the stick of the bow. This is counteracted by placing the small finger on the inner, flat side of the stick *just below the top ridge*. In this way, the little finger can feel secure as it adds its small pressure-control to the stroke (Illustration 29, and page 46, paragraph 3).

The collé stroke was introduced to us concurrently with the martelé stroke, because of the close relationship between the two. The initial suspension of the bow above the string is especially important in the collé. The finger action is similar to that of the martelé: curved to elongated on the down-stroke; elongated to curved on the up-stroke. The collé bowing is an extremely short, delicate, precise stroke and the bow comes off the string immediately upon completion of the finger motion (page 73). It concentrates on the clarity of the inset, or attack, of the tone.

Mr. Galamian recommended that the collé be practiced first on the *up-bow*. (The bow comes off the string more naturally after the up-stroke.) The bow is suspended slightly above the string and set silently "from the air." As the bow contacts the string, the fingers, in their elongated position, suddenly pinch the bow, assuming thereby a curved position. "In such a very short stroke as the collé, only the fingers are active" (page 74).
NOTE: The pinching of the bow on the up-stroke brings with it a very slight reaction in the form of an upward flick of the hand from the wrist. The bow leaves the string immediately. The result is a very short, very clear note. The collé is developed as a series of up-bows throughout the length of the bow. The suspension, re-setting of the bow on the string, and the

assuming of the elongated position of the fingers, precedes each up-stroke.

For the down-bow collé, starting at the frog, the fingers are curved only gently. The bow is again suspended and set, and the fingers move to their elongated position in performing the stroke. The hand drops very slightly from the wrist and the bow comes off the string. This down-stroke was also drilled in all sections of the bow. (See page 74, paragraphs 2 and 3.) Thereafter, "transportation" was added—one collé at the frog, the next at the point, the bow being carried in the air between the two strokes. When the fingers complete the down-stroke motion at the frog, they are then in position to perform the up-stroke at the point and vice versa. The goal is to produce exactly the same sound at both ends of the bow. As the precision of attack comes under control, we find a new clarity of sound in our overall playing, regardless of whether we are using martelé, détaché, or slurred bowings.

The reader will remember that Mr. Galamian also mentions the "broad collé" (Example 63, page 74, last paragraph). Here the arm joins in the short, fast stroke, giving breadth to the sound. It is very useful in a series of repeated chords, either up- or down-bow.

Practicing

The vehicle for the extensive development of the martelé was the Kreutzer Etude No. 7. The string crossings had to be accomplished with *absolute silence*, absolute control—no down-bow, up-bow jittering as the bow moved from one string to the next. The perpendicular motion of crossing strings was segregated from the horizontal motion of the drawing of the stroke. "The scratchy sound produced by too much pressure at the moment of stopping [in the martelé] or by the application of pressure too early before the next stroke should always be avoided" (page 71).

As soon as one note was played, the *bow*, as well as the fingers, had to be placed immediately on the new string and new note. "You must be on the new string at the end of the old stroke." Once this was accomplished, there could be a moment's pause before the new martelé stroke was initiated.

This way of working required the eyes to look ahead two notes and the mind to be fully prepared before the first note of the pair was played. In a short time we found, to our amazement, that our sight-reading ability was taking on a new efficiency, both in speed and in accuracy. Mr. Galamian had not told us that this would happen. He let us discover it for ourselves. This sense of discovery was mentioned by many students —one of the things that made our work with Mr. Galamian so very gratifying.

In the following discussion are listed, in sequential order, the most-often-recommended practice devices ("problems" or "variations") for the Kreutzer No. 7. Quoted practice rhythms bearing the boldface numbers (as **37**) are originally from the Galamian edition of Kreutzer's *Forty-two Etudes* (Copyright © 1963 by International Music Company, New York; used by permission). Some rhythms quoted here do not appear in that edition.

For bowing and martelé development we were instructed to "pause after each group of two (or three) notes" and "feel the 'pinch' in the bow before continuing." Practice devices include (a) half bow at the tip; (b) half bow at the frog; (c) down-down, up-up, stopping at the precise middle of the bow to readjust the bow-fingers each time; (d) two slurred, whole bow, and two separate, half bows; (e) the reverse of this, two separate first. Next, we were advised to use the *upper* two-thirds of the bow in a longer, faster stroke with the following rhythms (Example 95):

Example 95
Kreutzer: *Etude No. 7*

During all of this, it is important to preserve the "straightness" of the stroke as the point is approached. Mr. Galamian mentioned that the out motion was generally easier to acquire while performing the faster strokes.

The variations applied to this etude become a complete symposium on string crossings in every possible direction. The détaché also begins to enter the picture: "As the martelé is perfected, it will also add to the skill of the détaché." The two notes of the given octave are now played as shown in Example 96. Following any stop, the string is to be "caught" for a clean attack on the following note. We were told to group the notes first "in ⅜, then in ⅘, then by whole measures."

Example 96
Kreutzer: *Etude No. 7*

After these three-note groupings, groups of four were introduced, as given in Example 97. In slow practice, there was a disconnection at the end of each group of four notes.

Example 97
Kreutzer: *Etude No. 7*

Also:

When all of the variations were conquered satisfactorily, the patterns shown in Example 97 were to be played in sequence: first, martelé, stopping after each group; then détaché, faster, still making the stop; finally, continuously without stopping.

For breadth and richness in the broad détaché, the bow is applied full hair-surface on the string, between the middle and the point. "Feel as if the weight of the arm is hanging on the bow." As they became pertinent to the repertoire, the several varieties of détaché were introduced (see pages 67–69). One thinks of the Bach *Six Sonatas and Partitas* especially, in this connection.

There was also a Kreutzer No. 7 series to be played collé. The notes were used in *written order*, applying the collé as follows: (n) entirely at the frog, starting down or starting up; (o) entirely at the point, starting down or starting up; (p) with "transportation," frog, down, then point, up. The following rhythms, played with "a tiny, light movement," were then added (Example 98):

Example 98
Kreutzer: *Etude No. 7*

For these rhythms, we were told to "divide the bow into six and eight parts."

For further enlightenment, the reader is referred to the eight video tapes made in the studio at Meadowmount during the summers of 1979 and 1980. The first of the series (IG-1, Volume 1) shows Mr. Galamian teaching the collé and Martelé bowings as well as the scale system. Techniques for practicing Kreutzer No. 7 and Rode No. 1 are to be found in IG-5, Volume 5.*

---

* The other tapes in the series deal with repertoire. All are commercially available from Shar Music Company, 2465 S. Industrial Highway, Ann Arbor, Michigan, 48104.

The first few weeks of study were nothing less than grueling. This business of blasting the mind awake and putting it in control of the physical action was both mentally and physically tiring. For our practice, Mr. Galamian suggested a ten-minute break at the end of every hour to rest the mind. Four hours a day were considered sufficient.

During the development of the martelé with the finger action, the tip of the thumb became tender because of our concentrated efforts to get it to bend and recover properly at its middle joint. When we complained of a "sore thumb" we were greeted with laughter by the more experienced students. They, too, had gone through that stage. They comforted us with, "Great! Now you *know* you are on the right track. The thumb will get over it in another week," and it did. This thumb soreness was one of the transient prices of success. The acquired flexibility laid a foundation for many good things that happened later on in our playing. As our improvement became more noticeable, our spirits soared to new heights. We were gradually becoming recognizable as having studied with Mr. Galamian himself.

II. OTHER FACETS OF HIS TEACHING

In working with Mr. Galamian over a period of years on the first edition of this book, there were times when questions could be asked beyond the confines of the book itself. Some of these dealt with the training of the younger child. He stated his philosophy thus:

When you are dealing with the young student, there are occasions when you may think that it is time to present a certain technique. You find that it seems very difficult for the child. He is struggling. *Lay it aside!* Teach something else that he is *ready to learn.* In a month or so, try it again. Still it is extremely difficult. Again, lay it aside. The third time you come back to it—Ah! *Now* he is ready to encompass it. Go ahead and teach it!

In the book he remarks, "The teacher who takes his mission seriously will see in every single student an entirely new and challenging problem" (page 105). More than once we heard him say, "Every student has to be tailor made—custom built. . . . Some students respond to encouragement; some to a gentle, tactful handling; others to pressure with a heavy hand. The teacher has to find out which and then teach accordingly."

I asked Mr. Galamian about setting the left-hand position for the beginning student. "The fingers are the determining factor. They have to be placed in such a way as to allow them the most favorable conditions for their various actions. Once this is done, everything else—*thumb,* hand, arm—will find its corresponding natural position" (page 14, italics added). He asserted that "only what is natural is comfortable and efficient" (page 1), and that "a student who is uncomfortable with the instrument cannot express himself musically."

Mr. Galamian, then, was telling us to pay more attention to the fingers and a bit less to the thumb of the left hand. How do you start with the fingers? He answered the question thus, demonstrating as he spoke: "Locate the center point on the *tip* of the first-finger nail. With a pencil, draw a line from that point toward the center of the half-moon at the base of the nail. With the violin in playing position, this line will indicate the point of contact of the fleshy fingertip with the string. The line will stand up on the string as the player looks at it. The position of the thumb is then oriented to the fingers." With an amused smile he added, "After all, we do not play the notes with the thumb." NOTE: This position is shown from the player's point of view in Illustration 6, page 16. (In order to get a workable camera angle, the thumb had to be retracted toward the scroll. Therefore, disregard the position of the thumb in this picture.) For more about the thumb, see page 17, last paragraph, and page 18.

Galamian discusses the position of the elbow (page 13). He himself had long fingers. He showed us that when the elbow was too far to the right (under the violin), it forced the long fingers actually to curve under when they were placed on the string. "Naturalness is the first guiding principle."

Asked about "drill studies," such as those found in the Sevčik books, his reply was, "I cannot see how music and technique can be divorced from each other. Such reiterations are unmusical, and besides, they are boring to practice. It is far better to choose etudes that have some *musical* content and then to superimpose the technique on the etudes." He mentioned Wohlfahrt and Kayser for the less advanced player.

The Dont, *Twenty-four Exercises for the Violin,* Op. 37, formed part of his regular course of study and was used when students were ready for it. (Very often it followed on the heels of the Kreutzer No. 7 and before continuation with the complete Kreutzer.) Advanced students coming to Mr. Galamian for the first time also were often assigned the Dont Op. 37 exercises. For them, these studies provided a means of applying the various rhythms used for the A-major scale, as well as a chance for further development of the martelé and détaché bowings.

The first etude in Op. 37 (⅜ time signature, thirty-second notes, slurred twelve to the bar) is an excellent example of what we students called a "type study," an etude in which a whole mass of technique was built. The following bowings and rhythms from pages 97 and 98 were used: détaché unslurred throughout; slurred as written; spiccato. Also the rhythms were slurred by eights and by twelves for the left hand facility (Example 99).

Example 99
Dont: *Op. 37, Etude No. 1*

In the Dont Op. 37 studies, a most important principle emerged (Example 100): When the *up-bow preceded a slur,* the pressure was to be lessened and the *bow lifted from the string* at the end of the up-bow, thus eliminating the customary unpleasant crescendo, or scooping of the sound, so often heard (page 87, Example 74). This trained a certain lightness in the fast up-bow as the frog was approached. Later on, in speed work using the détaché, the lifting off ceased to exist but the lightness remained. For the fast down-bow before a slur, the out (forward) motion was imperative. This accommodation prevented the bow from slithering toward the fingerboard—a tendency it has in the fast down-stroke if compensation is not made. Further, the forward push turns the tip of the bow slightly in toward the bridge, adding a bit of pressure and a more solid sound on the beginning of the up stroke (Example 100). (Forward motion, middle to point.)

Example 100
Dont: *Op. 37, Etude No. 2,* beginning

The two techniques were applied throughout the book. It was up to the student to recognize where they were pertinent and to practice them without fail. During the performance of an etude in the lesson, Mr. Galamian would ask the student to change (after several lines of one variation) to another variation. Thus he checked on everything in a minimum amount of time, and, by the last double bar, knew exactly where the student had arrived in his progress.

Etudes that were written in four-note groupings were also to be practiced accenting in threes; three-note groupings, accenting in twos and fours. This shift of accent transformed any etude into an entirely different study. The eyes became more conscious of each written note *in its proper sequence,* and again sight-reading improved. Also the necessary repetition was built in and it was far from boring to practice.

In the double stop and chord studies, two-note groupings and rhythms were used in order to improve the rapid finger adjustments in setting the chords (♪. | ♪). Intonation also improved on the longer chord. A complete stop was made after the sustained chord each time. The shorter note was not played until the mind was "set" for both chords. (See Dont, Op. 37, No. 24, and Op. 35, No. 1.)

The reader is referred to the Glossary of Applied Techniques, pages 124–133, for further information.

One sometimes hears the muttered charge, "Galamian taught everybody in exactly the same way." Believe me, it is not true. What *is* true is that he understood the student's need to accomplish certain basic things if the highest degree of proficiency was to materialize eventually. If these things had not been conquered in the previous training, then they had to be done *now.* Mr. Galamian knew how to *"strengthen the link from mind to hands"*—the basic precept of his method. He produced results quickly and he *adapted everything to the individual student.* The logical sequence of his practice methods (and their results) was a source of wonder to us all. There was variety in the adaptations and in their application to the particular student.

Galamian spoke very little about himself—and never in the studio. There was no self-vaunting, which he detested, and he neither ridiculed nor made negative comments about other teachers. In the studio he spoke only about what had to be done and how to accomplish it. He never took a negative approach in his teaching: There were no lengthy discussions about what the student had done wrong; instead he would say, "Do this," or "Practice this way," and the trouble would be cured.

The course of study used the standard etude books: Kreutzer, *Forty-two Studies;* Fiorillo, *Thirty-six Studies or Caprices;* Rode, *Twenty-four Caprices;* Gaviniés, *Twenty-four Studies;* Dont, Op. 35, *Twenty-four Etudes and Caprices;* Dancla, Op. 73, *Twenty Brilliant and Characteristic Etudes;* and Wieniawski, Op. 10, *Ecole Moderne—Ten Etudes-Caprices.* The Dont, Op. 35, was the magnificent culmination of the practice methods. For this reason, it has been treated fully on pages 130–133. All except the Dancla are available in the Galamian edition, International Music Company, New York.

Thus far nothing has been said about the solo repertoire. Galamian taught all of the great concertos and concert solos. For the younger students on the way up, he used the customary works, including the Vivaldi *G minor Concerto*, the De Beriot and Rode concertos (6, 7, and 8, especially), and the Bach and Mozart concertos. "Interpretation is the final goal of all instrumental study, its only *raison d'être*. Technique is merely the means to this end, the tool to be used in the service of artistic interpretation" (page 6). But it was in the etudes that the technique was built.

There are several other aspects of the technical development that should be mentioned: the spiccato, the slurred staccato, general tonal development, intonation, and harmonics.

SPICCATO. For work on the spiccato, the Kreutzer No. 8 (E major etude) was often used. Using spiccato, each note was reiterated three times; then two times; finally, one time as written. (There are many practice variations suggested for the etude in the Galamian edition of Kreutzer.) Further development took place on Etude No. 10 (G major), which became the basis for one of his famous *symposiums*. The etude was first played martelé as written; then spiccato, each sixteenth-note three times with the bowing just as it came; next, twice on each sixteenth, lifting the bow off after the eighth note and starting the sixteenths down-bow each time; finally, using the down-bow, up-bow in normal sequence throughout the etude. At the end came the pay-off: changing the number of reiterations *in sequence* on the sixteenths (Example 101).

Example 101
Kreutzer: *Etude No. 8*

Mr. Galamian calls attention to the fact that the bow is dropped from the air for the spiccato (page 75) but that the sautillé fundamentally springs from the détaché stroke (page 77).

SLURRED STACCATO. The development of the on-the-string slurred staccato began with very slow practice. Each note was given the customary press-release attack as in the martelé, but *without the finger action developed in the Kreutzer Etude No. 7*. Instead, the second (middle) finger and the fourth (little) finger were removed from the stick of the bow (Illustration 35, page 80). This threw the press-release action into the proper muscles in the wrist and arm as the first finger applied the press-release through the pronation-supination motions of the lower arm. (The pressure is applied while the bow is standing still, and released as the bow moves.) As far as I know, this removing of the two fingers from the bow was unique with Mr. Galamian's teaching. It solved the problem for more than one student.

Noted on my study copy of the Wieniawski *Ecole*, Etude No. 4, "Le Staccato" are the following instructions from Mr. Galamian: "For slow practice, press while stopping but conserve bow on the release. Remove second and fourth fingers from the bow. . . . Do not let the fingers control here." NOTE: The scratchy sound youngsters often produce in the slurred staccato is due to their adding pressure (often excessively) *after* the bow starts to move, instead of pressing while it is standing still.

TONE QUALITY. It was the exception to the rule if a student did not show noticeable improvement in tone quality early in his work with Mr. Galamian. As the lessons progressed, we were made efficiently conscious of the interaction of the *three* factors influencing tone quality: speed of stroke, pressure of bow, and distance from the bridge. This last, Galamian called the "sounding point." (Refer to pages 55–61.) The experimental exercises given on page 60, starting with paragraph two, were part of our instruction.

We learned also that a certain freedom of bowing is necessary when playing the very highest notes of the violin's range. Mr. Galamian often re-marked the bowing in such passages in order to give sufficient bow for the required richness and beauty of sound. As in all tonal work, the ear is the final judge. On the playing of sustained high notes, "Avoid sudden extra pressure in the middle of the bow. It causes the high tones to crack. . . . Also, use a free vibrato, not a 'white' tone." Placing more of the fleshy fingertip on the string while playing the highest notes was also recommended for certain students.

INTONATION. Any slight discrepancy was instantly pounced upon, "C sharp!" "E flat!" and we would go back and correct it. He advised concerning intonation, "When practicing for intonation, disregard other things. Concentrate on the intonation." Then, with a gleeful smile, half seriously, half humorously, "After all, instant adjustment is also part of the technique."

HARMONICS. Mr. Galamian told us to bow harmonics near the bridge: "Use the same amount of bow-pressure and bow-speed that you would use if you were playing an open string with the bow moving at that particular sounding-point. . . . For the fast slide to the very high harmonic, press the finger into the string a bit (a scooping motion) just before arriving at the harmonic," for security and sound.

I cannot remember that Mr. Galamian ever had to refer to the printed music unless he was marking a fingering in our own part. Everything, etudes included, was in his head. During the lesson *he concentrated his full attention on the student's performance*, analyzing, judging, adapting the editing to improve that student's rendition. Never was a teacher more dedicated to his pupils. His excuse for not doing other things was, "But the students *need* the lessons."

To end this long technical discussion, I would like to make a personal comment. The Galamian method of working was the first practice method I had ever experienced where I realized that every facet of the playing was being drilled, and was moving ahead, *simultaneously*, during the practice hour—mind, ears, eyes, physical control of the hands and of the instrument, intonation, tone, bow control, sight-reading, and left hand facility. It was mind-boggling. Fifteen minutes of "Galamian practice" was worth an hour spent in any other kind of technical study. "Once the technique is built and is secure, an hour a day is all you need to keep it there." This, too, I found to be true.

Somewhere along the way someone asked, "Is your method essentially Russian, or is it French?" He answered, "Partly Russian, partly French, and a good deal of my own."

Asked about his teaching career, he said, "One must make a choice—either a solo career or a teaching career. You cannot do both equally well. One or the other will suffer. . . . Ever since I was a child I have been interested in the *how*-to-do-it aspect. After some time as a soloist I found that I was successful as a teacher and that I *preferred* teaching."

One student asked, "When there are so many fantastic violinists, why is it that so few of them become world famous as soloists?" Mr. Galamian's thoughtful reply to this question follows:

It is because, to become world famous, talent and genius are not enough. One has to be endowed with a brilliant mind that can work like lightning; with an ability to concentrate for long periods of time; with the personal drive, will power, and perseverance to do the necessary years of preparation; and with the hands and innate muscular qualities of flexibility that make possible the brilliant technique required. Further, musicality, the fine ear, must be innate; the personality should have appeal for the universal audience, and a high degree of personal magnetism must be present to carry the audience along, musically and emotionally. There must be musical understanding, creativeness, and imagination in the interpretation. It is only rarely in a generation that all of these things come together in one person. The lack of any single factor *may* prevent the achieving of world-renowned status.

Those of us who studied at length with Mr. Galamian subscribe to his dictum: "The building of violin technique is no longer a matter of trial and error. It is now an *exact science*."

III. A GLOSSARY OF APPLIED VARIATIONS

Any reader of this book, making the effort to apply the methods to his own work, must do so conscientiously and wholeheartedly. He must realize that the method is one thing; *how* it is executed is something else. Unless the execution matches in perfection the method itself, the results will be less than acceptable.

If Mr. Galamian speaks of a bent thumb, the thumb must be *bent*. Flexibility of a joint means just that. An unshrugged shoulder is an unshrugged shoulder. Mr. Galamian never asked for the impossible. Nor did he ask every student to apply variations that the student had already mastered. Something more difficult would be assigned instead. As one of his fine students remarked, "Mr. Galamian is *demanding* and *consistent*."

In the following pages will be found many references to two basic rhythms: (a) ♩. ♪ (♩ ⅞ ♪) and (b) ♪♪. (♪♪ ⅞). They have a built-in magic. Bowed separately, using the sixteenth rest, there is opportunity to set the bow for clarity of attack on the following sixteenth note—bowing and coordination skills. Used as left-hand rhythms in slurs of many notes, they build left-hand speed accompanied by relaxation. Using *a*, the speed occurs on the second to third notes (sixteenth to eighth), the fourth and fifth notes, and so on. Using *b*, the speed occurs between the first and second notes, then the third and fourth notes, and continuing. Thus speed has been trained between *every pair of notes*. The dotted note serves as a moment of relaxation following the fast sixteenth. When the passage is conquered with the rhythms, the subsequent performance as written shows improvement in both speed and accuracy.

The addition of rhythms *c*, *d*, *e*, and *f* from page 97 adds further speed to the fingers since now four fast motions have to be made before the moment of relaxation occurs. Again speed, control, correlation (page 6, footnote), and security become evident. The ear hears every note of the passage highlighted as a longer note. The practice may be done with separate bows or with slurs superimposed.

The practice assignments are given *in toto* for two books of etudes: Dont, Op. 37, for less advanced players, and Dont, Op. 35, for technically accomplished performers. On the pages between these two outlines, the etudes from the standard books are classified under several headings; under each heading the general practice techniques applicable to that classification are followed by a list of the pertinent etudes.

Mr. Galamian reminds us, "The combinations [rhythms and bowings] are by no means complete or exhaustive. . . . The goal is not merely to play all of the possible combinations, but rather to master a few new ones each day so as to improve and to perfect gradually the coördination and correlation."

Dont, Op. 37, Twenty-four Exercises

NOTE: In this outline, a dot over/under a note signifies martelé; a long line signifies détaché. In general, martelé is used for the slower practice, détaché for the faster renditions. (The numbers at the left refer to the etude numbers.)

1. See pages 118–119 for a full discussion of this etude.
2. See pages 119–120 for a discussion of this etude. Also, practice it slowly in martelé, faster in détaché accenting in twos, in threes, in fours, first deleting all slurs, later with slurs as written still retaining the varieties of accentuation. The bow comes *off* the string *after* an *up-bow before a slur*. Bow hand pushes *out* on a *down-bow before a slur*. Apply here and throughout the book. Add:

   These two rhythms are practiced unslurred for the bowing, then slurring six notes for left hand control.
3. Separate bows, unslurred: first at the point; then at the frog. Play it spiccato. Rhythms:

   Use a clean attack on the sixteenth notes. The following, unslurred, then later slurring in sixes and as written. Keep the right thumb bent.

4. Martelé on the staccato notes, slurred as written; then, same, détaché.
5. Unslurred martelé; unslurred détaché; slurred as written.
6. Same as No. 2 above.
7. Unslurred martelé; unslurred détaché; unslurred spiccato. Slurred as written using martelé; same, détaché.

8. Unslurred martelé; unslurred détaché. Slurred by half-measures. As written. "Pay attention to the dynamics."

9. Unslurred détaché, first starting down-bow, then starting up-bow; spiccato, first starting down-bow, then starting up-bow. Practice the whole etude at the point of the bow. Finally, as written, first measure starting down-bow, second measure starting up-bow, and so on.

10. As written, martelé with *broad slurs*.

11. As written. Stop bow momentarily before the grace notes and "catch" them.

12. As written; détaché; Viotti stroke (); spiccato.

13. Unslurred détaché, first starting down-bow, then starting up-bow; spiccato, first starting down-bow, then starting up-bow. See Example 102: Bow entire study each way.

Example 102
Dont: *Op. 37, No. 13*

Finally, slurred as written.

14. As written, middle of bow. Follow marked fingerings.

15. As written. Special fingerings, measure 12, 1-3-1-4, 2-1-4-2, 1-2-4-2; and fourth measure from the end, 3-2-0-2, 1-0-4-2, 3-1-2-4.

16. Unslurred middle; unslurred détaché; as written.

17. As written—for one-finger shifts.

18. Unslurred, martelé; détaché. As double stops, grouping the notes in pairs; unslurred, spaced between strokes. Finally, slurred as written.

19. As written. Measures 7 and 8, and similar places, slur in fours on the sixteenth notes; in twos on the eighth notes.

20. Separate bows, middle. Staccatos on, also off, string.

21. Same as No. 20. Also slur in fours.

22. Slur by twos; as written.

23. Martelé; détaché; as written.

24. "Drop" bow on middle note so all three notes sound together. "Suspend" before the drop. Martelé, all down-bow throughout. Also use down–up as it comes.

Eventually the rhythms and bowings quoted here in Part Three become too easy. ("The player has to present the mind-muscle unit with . . . problems that proceed from the simple to the ever more complex" (page 6). Thus the need arises for more challenging problems. At that time we begin combining a rhythmic problem from Section 2, page 97, with a bowing problem from Section 4, page 98—two problems at one time! The imagination is further challenged to "create its own problems," and to "master a few new ones each day."

Classification of Etudes

   I.   Written throughout in notes of equal value, unslurred.
  II.   Same as Type I, but slurred by full measures.
 III.   Separately bowed notes interspersed with short slurs. Mixed bowings.
  IV.   Double stops and chord studies.
   V.   String crossings emphasized: (a) in martelé; (b) with wrist action; (c) with finger action.
  VI.   Varied as to technical requirements, mixed techniques.

Full titles of the etude books are found on page 120.

TYPES I AND II. For slow practice, martelé, unslurred. For faster practice, détaché, unslurred. Apply the two basic rhythms: ♩♩ and ♪♩. (♪♪♩ | ♩♪𝄾). Same rhythms slurred in 8s and 12s. Rhythmic accuracy stressed. Harder problems, separately bowed or slurred:

Accenting in threes, use:

(In the following list, numbers in parentheses refer to etudes for which these techniques are only partially applicable.)

	Unslurred Etudes (Type I)	*Etudes in Long Slurs* (Type II)
Dont, Op. 37:	none.	1, 3, 5, 8, 11, 13, 16–18, 21.
Kreutzer:	2, 5, 8, 12.	9, (14), 23 cadenzas, 29, (34).
Fiorillo:	11, 21, 34, (35).	Some places in 8, 19, 32.
Rode:	Half of 1, 4, 9; 8, 10.	3, 12, (13), 14, 16, 20, (23).
Dont, Op. 35:	*(See full discussion following on pp. 130–133.)*	
Dancla:	4, 15.	2, (5), 6, 8, 9, 13, 17, 19.
Wieniawski:	none.	2, (3), 6 at Poco piu, (7).

TYPE III. Short slurs among separately bowed notes. Practice unslurred, martelé. Then martelé with slurs inserted as written. Same with détaché, faster. Use rhythms in threes and fours as in Types I and II. Be mindful of the bowing "lift off" and "out" before slurs (page 119). For etudes written in groups of threes, accent also in twos and fours; those written in fours, accent in threes. Stress continuity of dynamic between slurred and unslurred notes (Example 37, page 56; Example 73, page 86). (Numbers in parentheses indicate that the technique is partially applicable.)

Dont, Op. 37:	2, 4, 6, 7, 10, 14, 15.
Kreutzer:	3, 26, 30, (31), 37.
Fiorillo:	Sections of 2, 6, 7, 9, 10, 12, 27, (29), 31, (33).
Rode:	2 in martelé; 6 at Moderato, 15, 17, 18, 22, 24 Agitato.
Gaviniés:	(2), all other etudes in the book except 1, 3, 12, 15. In fast tempo, the lift off between slurs is omitted, but lightness remains.
Dont, Op. 35:	(2) 13.
Dancla:	16.
Wieniawski:	(1) (5).

TYPE IV. Double stops and three- and four-note chords. For double stops, use martelé and détaché, unslurred. Slur by twos, etc. For rhythms applied to double stops, see Dont, Op. 35, Etudes 8, 12, 14, 16, 18 (pages 130–133); also Op. 37, Etudes 18, 19, 22 (page 126). For chords, see discussion of Dont, Op. 35, No. 1, page 130.

Kreutzer:	32, 33, 34, 35, 36. On 34, the rhythms given for Types I and II above in the four-note patterns were suggested by Mr. Galamian ("a number of measures done each way").
Fiorillo:	Rhythms for training fast finger changes—4, 17, 18.
Rode:	16 "Skip it," 23 as written.
Gaviniés:	Use 12 as double stops. 15 as is.
Dancla:	3 in "crisp spiccato." "Drop bow on string in *mf*, catch string in *piano*." In 6, 11, 12, and 20, apply rhythms to double-stop passages.
Wieniawski:	3.

TYPE V. String Crossings, three categories:
(a) *Notes of equal value unslurred.* Martelé.

Kreutzer:	7 (see discussion, pp. 114–116), part of 30.
Fiorillo:	30.

Rode: 1 at moderato, 2, a section of 21.
Gaviniés: 19, 20, part of 22.
Dont, Op. 35:   5.

(b) *Flexible wrist crossings.* In general, middle of bow or middle to point. Bowed separately or slurred. Develop wrist by using hand turned *up* from wrist for lower string on down-bow (inner edge of bow hair); hand dropped below wrist for upper string on up-bow (outer edge of hair). Wrist motion can also be applied in long slurs for smooth crossings to neighboring strings—very subtle here. Galamian mentions "wrist" in the following etudes:

Kreutzer: 9 (see below), 13.
Fiorillo: 20, 23 (also change it to a four-note group as
                         follows: lower A, E, higher A, add E on the
                         D string, and slur in twos), 24 (same varia-
                         tions as 23), 29, some places in 25 and 30,
                         36 (1 through 7).
Rode: 18.
Gaviniés: 4, 13, 14, sections of 19.
Dont, Op. 35:   5, 7, 13.

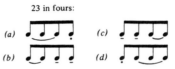

23 in fours:

(c) *Finger crossings.* "At the frog, crossings are made by the fingers. They are curved on the lower string, straightened on the upper string. (Motion described on page 78, Illustration 27, "Vertical Motion of the Fingers.") NOTE: The little finger is active here, pressing to tilt the bow to the upper string, relaxing for the lower string. The "Type Study" was the Kreutzer No. 9. Mr. Galamian had us use the first five lines, fingered throughout so that each pair of notes crossed strings. (In measure 9, third position; measure 10, first position, etc.) The following problems were set up, slurred by measures (Example 103).

Example 103
Kreutzer: *Etude No. 9*

In using the long slurs, the finger-crossing was made at the frog. This gradually became wrist-crossing as the middle of the bow was neared. Can be applied to the following etudes.

Kreutzer: 9.
Gaviniés: 12.

TYPE VI. Etudes requiring varied techniques within the single study. Apply the several variations to any small section where they would be pertinent to improve that section. Samples of such etudes are:

Fiorillo:	1, 2, 13, 32, 35.
Rode:	5, 6, 7, 11, 13, 20.
Gaviniés:	1, 3, 15, 23, 24.
Dancla:	6, 7, 10, 11, 20.
Wieniawski, Op. 10:	1–10 (for mastery of all that has gone before).

Dont, Op. 35, Twenty-four Etudes and Caprices

The numbers at the left refer to the etude numbers.

1. Down-bow, up-bow, breaking the chords; vibrato. First finger off the string for the vibrato. Down, down, throughout. Drop bow on three strings simultaneously. Rhythms: ♩. ♫ and ♫. ♩. Group chords in twos, in threes, etc. for acquiring left-hand dexterity. Same, down–up throughout. ♫ ♫♫

2. When *forte*, use détaché; when *piano*, spiccato. Consider the "condensation" of the tone—pressure or not on the first finger on the bow.

3. For shoulder relaxation, play this study entirely *at the frog*. Détaché and unslurred. Play very broadly in détaché. Spiccato—not so much finger action. In spiccato, "catch" the rebound—"starch" in the fingers. Also use spiccato on two notes, sautillé on four notes thus: ♩ ♩ ♫♫♫ Slur the study in eights and in sixteens. Finally, "bow this one for yourself, using bowings from the A-major scale" (page 98). (We were expected to make the result as musical and interesting as possible.) Also, 2-6 (*saut.*)-4-2-2.

4. "As if each chord had a dot over it." Practice articulating collé on each half of the chord, then on the whole chord. Work for smoothness on the three-note chord—not too near the bridge. "Don't anticipate the articulation. Articulate and then sustain. The softer you want the chord, the farther from the frog you start it. At the ricochet, use bow-fingers for the first note, then let the bow carry on from there. Nearer the frog [closer to the middle of the bow] for slow ricochet practice, nearer the point for fast playing." NOTE: Mr. Galamian is stressing here that the bow bounces faster the closer to the point it is when dropped on the string. Speed of the ricochet depends on distance from the frog.

5. Détaché, ♩. = 60. Slurred by half-measures, ♩ = 50. A sharp attack throughout as written. Wrist flexible for the crossings. On inner edge of hair for down-bow on lower string (hand slightly above wrist); outer edge for up-bow

on upper string (hand a bit below wrist). "The alternation of edges of bow-hair helps the sound and the attack." Bow stays close to both strings. "Don't reach too far front for this. The motion from edge to edge serves the same purpose. . . . Use this slurring (𝅘𝅥 𝅘𝅥 𝅘𝅥), but *not* as triplets—accent *only* the first of the six notes as written."

6. Intonation! Play as triplets throughout. (See Example 104.)

Example 104
Dont: *Op. 35, Etude No. 6*

Short, light. "Play several lines using left hand pizzicato, alternating down bow, up bow on the first note of the three, pizzicato on the second and third notes. Short trills, like pizzicato for the left hand. Don't strike the fingers. It is the lifting off of the finger that makes the trill." See page 30, Example 18.

7. This etude is for position of the left hand. The *following* note determines whether it is a shift or not. Slow practice, smooth sound, use wrist. Use separate bows, also slurs, as written. "Sound!"

8. Rhythms: See Example 105.

Example 105
Dont: *Op. 35, Etude No. 8*

9. In sections, slurred, played double forte (a few notes at a time). Stop the bow before the trill. Pay attention to the *sound* of the note preceding the trill. Do not lengthen the trill. Lift bow off before the chord.

10. *Double forte* at the frog. Use down–up. Drop bow on string for the down stroke. Use wrist. Mark the changes in harmony. For piano, play between middle and frog.

11. Start the chord here a little way from the frog. Use a faster bow on the three-note chords. When playing the double stops (measure 2, etc.), articulate them but sustain them beautifully.

12. Intonation! Make the forte really sound. Use 𝅘𝅥. 𝅘𝅥 and 𝅘𝅥𝅮. to make the interval of the fourth sound simultaneously. Rhythms: 𝅘𝅥𝅮𝅘𝅥𝅮𝅘𝅥 ‖ 𝅘𝅥𝅮𝅘𝅥𝅮 𝅘𝅥𝅯𝅘𝅥𝅯𝅘𝅥𝅯𝅘𝅥𝅯 Group in fours, starting on the first note of the sixteenths, the eighths being changed to sixteenths. (Sustain the quarter note.) Make a definite start on the first of the sixteenth notes.

13. A broad, straight stroke. Also spiccato. See that wrist is used in the slurred string crossings. In spiccato, a balance between sharpness and distance (length of stroke).

14. Use rhythms for intonation and facility in thirds. Make it *sound*. "In slow practice, exaggerate the highness of the lower note in places where two fingers touch each other on neighboring strings." (See third double stop, for example, a "half-step placing" of the fingers on neighboring strings.) "Such finger placings tend to spread when playing fast in double stops." Slur in fours, slow tempo.

15. First, down–up, down–up, without the trills, using whole bow. Next, slur without the trills, still using whole bow, down followed by up. Down, up, unslurred, using the trills. Finally, as written. "Approach the upper note. Give it a little color by not shortening it too much." NOTE: This is the famous study where Mr. Galamian offered a dollar to anyone who could perform it without missing a single note in intonation. Michael Rabin was the one who got the dollar!

16. Hard spiccato at the frog. Practice in slow legato, slurring in threes. Again, increase the sharpness of the notes raised by accidentals (in slow practice). Articulate with length in the stroke as in a sautillé stroke. "You have to exaggerate the highness of sharped notes in patterns where the fingers touch when practicing slowly. This 'sharpness' will not sound sharp in fast tempo."

17. The slides "well lubricated. Mark the note before the slide. Lighten the finger while sliding—the thumb makes the slide." Second measure, A to F, "Make the shift with the whole arm. Keep hand and fingers in the same relative position." "The speed of the shift itself is proportional to the speed of the execution of the notes. In practicing slower, shift slower. If shifts are made rapidly in slow tempo, they sound more, are more noticeable—stick out. . . . Use sufficient bow for the highest notes to increase the beauty of their sound." For speeding up, use ♩. ♫♪

18. First, as written. Next, heavy spiccato at the frog, forte, with a good drop on each note. Third, play it like a cadenza. See Example 106.

Example 106
Dont: Op. 35, Etude No. 18

19. Détaché, marking the printed accent. Separate bows with articulate spiccato, lower part of the bow. Slurred spiccato

by fours. "It is not necessary to exaggerate, or even to use this accent in slurred spiccato. (See *flying spiccato*, page 81.) Answer to question: "The wrist is not used [as given in the No. 5 etude] for this type of string crossing in spiccato."

20. For connection of tone and notes. Make it sound "connected." Use plenty of bow. Feel "starch" in the fingers (not too flexible here). "Feel the rosin of the bow in the fingers themselves." "Keep left hand fingers in same relative position in the shifts." "For slow practice in the sustained sound, slow down the bow toward the end of each stroke."

21. "Work this one out for yourself."

22. "Play as written, *even in slow practice, for bow control.* (Also applied in Dancla No. 2 and No. 6 etudes.) Stop before the trill. Don't "swallow" the note before the stop. See that it "sounds" rich and full.

23. "In the 'broken chord,' the three notes of the chord should sound simultaneously. Use a small amount of bow with intensity of sound on the sixteenth notes—not broadly on them . . . 'concentrate' the sound of the sixteenths."

24. "Skip it."

Practice Suggestions for Dancla and Wieniawski

DANCLA. No. 13. "Practice these measures with *bowed rhythms* to perfect the correlation between bow and left hand." No. 17: Use rhythms. Skip 18. Etude No. 19: "Wrist used in string crossings if articulation of crossing-note is to match articulation of fingers. For smoothness of effect, do NOT use the wrist motion for the crossings."

WIENIAWSKI. No. 1: Sautillé. "Practice with only first finger and thumb on bow. Thumb very flexible. Détaché, same, going over into sautillé." No. 2: "Keep always on the slow side for bow control. Continue the feeling of more tone, solidity or compactness of sound." Same in No. 3. No. 8: "Work for complete *sound* in the slower tempo." "Lift bow after the first chord, 'whipping' the attack on the second chord" (page 69, etc.)

Vita
IVAN GALAMIAN

1903	Born in Tabriz, Persia (now Iran), on January 23, old calendar (February 5, present calendar).
ca. 1904	Family moved to Moscow.
1919	Graduated at age 16 from the School of the Philharmonic Society in Moscow, where he was a student of Professor Mostrass. Moved to Paris where he studied privately with Lucien Capet.
1925–29	Faculty member, Russian Conservatory in Paris.
1937	Came to the United States for the first time.
1941	Married Judith Johnson in New York City.
1944	Founded Meadowmount Summer Violin School, in Westport, N.Y. (near Elizabethtown); served as director of the school until his death in 1981.
1944–81	Faculty, Curtis Institute of Music, Philadelphia.
1946–81	Faculty, Julliard School of Music, New York City.
1954	Honorary doctorate, Curtis Institute.
1965	Honorary member, Royal Academy of Music, London.
1966	Honorary degree, Oberlin College.
1966	Master Teacher Award, American String Teachers Association.
1968	Honorary degree, Cleveland College of Music.
1981	Died in New York City.

PUBLICATIONS BY IVAN GALAMIAN

In addition to the etude books mentioned on page 120, the following Galamian editions are available.

BACH, *Concerto No. 1 (A Minor)*. New York: International Music Company, 1960.

——, *Concerto No. 2 (E Major)*. New York: International Music Company, 1960.

——, *Six Sonatas and Partitas for Violin Alone*. New York: International Music Company, 1971. (Includes facsimile of the original Bach Mss.)

BRAHMS, *Sonatas, Op. 78, Op. 100, Op. 108*. New York: International Music Company.

BRUCH, *Scottish Fantasy, Op. 46*. New York: International Music Company, 1975.

CONUS, *Concerto in E Minor*. New York: International Music Company, 1976.

DONT, *Twenty-four Etudes and Caprices, Op. 35*. New York: International Music Company, 1968.

——, *Twenty-four Exercises, Op. 37*. New York: International Music Company, 1967.

DVORAK, *Concerto in A Minor, Op. 53*. New York: International Music Company, 1975.

FIORILLO, *Thirty-six Studies or Caprices*. New York: International Music Company, 1964.

GALAMIAN (with NEUMANN), *Contemporary Violin Technique*, Part I, Scale and Arpeggio Exercises; Part II, Double and Multiple Stops. New York: Galaxy Music Company, 1963 and 1966.

GAVINIÉS, *Twenty-four Studies*. New York: International Music Company, 1963.

KREUTZER, *Forty-two Etudes*. New York: International Music Company, 1963.

MAZAS, *Etudes Speciales, Op. 36, Part 1*. New York: International Music Company, 1964.

——, *Etudes Brilliantes, Op. 36, Part 2*. New York: International Music Co., 1972.

PAGANINI, *Twenty-four Caprices*. New York: International Music Company, 1973.

RODE, *Twenty-four Caprices*. New York: International Music Company, 1962.

SAINT-SAENS, *Caprice, Op. 52, No. 6*. New York: International Music Company, ND.

SINDING, *Suite in A Minor, Op. 10*. New York: International Music Company, 1970.

TCHAIKOVSKY, *Three Pieces, Op. 42*. New York: International Music Company, 1977.

VIVALDI, *Concerto in A Minor, F.1, 170*. New York: International Music Company, 1956.

——, *Concerto in G Minor, Op. 12, No. 1*. New York: International Music Company, 1973.

——, *Concerto for Two Violins, (D Minor), Op. 3, No. 11*. New York: International Music Company, 1964.

——, *Concerto for Two Violins, (A Minor), F.1—177*. Piccioli-Galamian, New York: International Music Company, 1956.

VIEUXTEMPS, *Concerto No. 5 in A Minor, Op. 37*. New York: International Music Company, 1957.

WIENIAWSKI, *Concerto No. 2 in D Minor, Op. 22*. New York: International Music Company, 1957.

——, *Ecole Moderne, Op. 10*. New York: International Music Company, 1973.

INDEX

INDEX
TO MUSICAL EXAMPLES

APPLIED RHYTHMS AS GIVEN IN THE POSTSCRIPT